UNLOCKING SECRETS
IN THE
SECOND COMING
SCROLLS

UNLOCKING SECRETS
IN THE

SECOND COMING
SCROLLS

Searching for the Time of Christ's Return
PERRY STONE, JR

Voice of Evangelism
Phone: (423) 478-3456
Fax: (423) 478-1392
www.perrystone.org

ISBN: 0-9708611-2-5
Library of Congress Control Number: 2003115838
Copyright 2004 by Voice of Evangelism, Inc.
P.O. Box 3595
Cleveland, TN 37320
(423) 478-3456

Printed in the United Stated of America

Dedication

With warmest regards, I dedicate
this book to all believers
who are anticipating and looking for the glorious
appearing of our Lord and Savior, Jesus Christ
(Titus 2:13).

May the research information
and Biblical truth written in this book encour-
age you to continue anticipating that great day
of redemption (Luke 21:28).

CONTENTS

But you, Daniel, shut up the words,

and seal the book until the time of

the end; many shall run to and fro,

and knowledge shall increase

(Daniel 12:4).

PREFACE

The "time of the end" is not the end of time. Believers often comment about how close we are to the end of time, an apocalyptic expression indicating the closing days before Christ returns. However, time does not actually end when Christ returns. The moment His feet touch the Mount of Olives begins the first day of a 1,000-year reign (Zechariah 14:4; Revelation 20:3). Satan will then be confined to the dark abyss while the world enjoys 1,000 years of peace, liberated from Satan, the father of tyrants (Revelation 20:1-5). Therefore, the end of time is an incorrect interpretation of a prophetic term.

Daniel was the Hebrew prophet who expressed the term "time of the end." According to Daniel 12:4, the scroll of Daniel was to be sealed until the *time of the end*. The angelic messenger indicated that Daniel's prophecies would be understood at the time of the end, when the events recorded in Daniel's scroll begin to come to pass. Then "knowledge would be increased." All Biblical prophecy can best be interpreted as it is being fulfilled. As events unfold, the meaning of the predictions becomes clear. Studying prophecy gives believers a strong foundation in which to build a case and prove the Bible is true because its prophecies are coming to pass.

Over 600 years after Daniel's visions, the apostle John received a series of supernatural visitations in the form of visions and penned the famous Apocalypse, the last book in the English Bible, called the Book of Revelation. The vision in the Apocalypse is a continuation of the Book of Daniel. However, when John concluded the 33 sections of the Book of Revelation, his angelic messenger commanded him, "Do not seal the words of the prophecy of this book, for the time is at hand" (Revelation 22:10).

Why was Daniel instructed to seal his vision until the time of the end, then 600 years later, John was commanded not to seal his book? I believe there were three reasons:

- ♦ Daniel's prophecies were a message for Israel, Jerusalem, and the Jewish people (Daniel 9:24, 10:14). John's apocalyptic message was revealed to the church during the dispensation of God's grace (Ephesians 1:10; 3:1-4).

- ♦ John was to send his book to the seven main churches located in Asia Minor. Thus, his message had to be opened, copied and distributed for the church's sake.

- ♦ Daniel's prophecies would be better understood after John received his vision recorded in the Book of Revelation. Thus, when the information in both prophetic books is studied together, a picture of end-time events can be understood.

A special blessing is placed upon those who read and keep the words in the Book of Revelation: "Behold, I am coming quickly! Blessed is he who keeps the words of the prophecy of this book" (Revelation 22:7). Daniel's revelation cannot be completely understood without the Book of Revelation.

The combined visions from both ancient scrolls give a clear picture of future events. Daniel's revelation was given to Israel, while John's vision was marked for the Christian church. Daniel revealed the future of world empires that would dominate the Jewish people. Many of Daniel's later prophecies could only be understood as they came to pass, thus the "words were sealed until the time of the end." John's vision was to be opened and read to the churches in his day.

For centuries, Rabbis have unrolled ancient prophetic scrolls to gain perspective into the symbolism and mysteries of the ancient text. Modern scholars and students of prophecy are consistently examining the prophetic scriptures, and many are suggesting we may be the generation that will see most of the major end time prophecies come to pass (Matthew 24:34).

With the Holy Spirit's illumination, I will unlock ancient Biblical predictions to determine if certain Biblical prophecies are coming to pass; and if so, whether they are pointing to the soon return of Jesus. I will endeavor to provide accurate and current information to confirm the presentation.

Before Christ's first appearance, anointed prophets searched the scrolls to determine the manner of Messiah's appearance (1 Peter 1:10, 11). In this book, I will follow that tradition and use the Biblical text, along with history and present-day events, to search for the time of Messiah's second coming (Acts 1:9-11).

Of this salvation the prophets have in-

quired and searched carefully, who proph-

esied of the grace that would come to you,

searching what, or what manner of time,

the Spirit of Christ which was in them was

indicating when He testified beforehand

the sufferings of Christ and the glories that

would follow (1 Peter 1:10, 11).

Introduction

The Hebrew prophets, whose visions, dreams and revelations were penned on ancient parchments, were a divinely inspired company of men. From the visions of Ezekiel at the river Chebar in Babylon to the Hebrew captive Daniel, who walked the halls of Nebuchadnezzar's palaces, these holy men inscribed history, often thousands of years before it happened.

These prophecies are the major difference between the Christian faith and all other religions. It is the scrutiny and fulfillment of Bible prophecy which proves that Christ was the true Messiah and that He will return to set up His earthly kingdom in Jerusalem (Psalm 2:6, Zechariah 9:9).

According to the apostle Peter, the anointed prophets who wrote the prophecies on parchments received bits and pieces of information concerning the first coming of the Messiah. Like a large jigsaw puzzle with many pieces, they were unable to match the pieces to form a perfect picture. As Peter indicates, these inspired men were diligently searching and comparing one another's prophecies to unlock the timing of the Messiah's appearance.

The Holy Spirit revealed that the Hebrew Messiah would be born in Bethlehem (Micah 5:2) and come from the tribe of Judah (Genesis 49:10). The prophets were shown that Christ would be born of a virgin (Isaiah 7:14), and that He would appear in the geographical region of Galilee of the Gentiles (Isaiah 9:1, 2).

Even the prophet David foresaw the "suffering Messiah" in Psalm 22 when he wrote that His (Messiah's) hands and feet would be pierced (Psalm 22:16), and that lots would be cast for His garments (Psalm 22:18). Psalm 22 lists seven major prophecies that were fulfilled at the crucifixion of Christ

Psalm 22	The Fulfillment
My God why have You forsaken Me?	Matthew 27:46
He trusted God; let Him deliver Him.	Matthew 27:43
I am slain as a sacrifice.	Hebrews 9:26
They pierce My hands and My feet.	John 19:37
Gambling for My garments	Matthew 27:35
Men are mocking Me.	Matthew 27:29
My tongue cleaves to My mouth.	Matthew 27:48

It should also be noted that the future plan of redemption was hidden in major events in the Old Testament. These events were pictures, or types and shadows, of what would come. As far back as Genesis 22:1, 2, when Abraham offered Isaac on Mount Moriah, we see the picture of God the Father who would one day offer His Son on the cross at the same location (Mount Moriah in Jerusalem), where Abraham laid his son upon the altar!

The Hebrew nation sacrificed many lambs during the first Passover, placing three marks of blood on the left, right, and upper posts of their doors (Exodus 12:7). This procedure was a perfect picture of the day when Jesus Christ, the Lamb of God, would die near the time of Passover, and three crosses would be erected on a hill in Jerusalem. Christ's cross was in the middle and two other crosses were on His left and right sides (John 19:17-18).

I believe every Hebrew prophet studied the predictions of the prophets who came before them, just as Daniel, in Babylon, unrolled the scroll of Jeremiah to read his predictions alluding to the Jewish captivity in Babylon (Daniel 9:2). Each Hebrew seer had bits and pieces of the picture, but none saw clearly until the event itself came to pass.

THE SECOND COMING

The miracles of Christ's ministry demonstrated that He was the expected Messiah. Ancient prophecies told of a Messianic kingdom in which the king Messiah would rule from Jerusalem (Daniel 7:27; Zechariah 14). Months before Christ's death, resurrection and ascension, the disciples inquired about this kingdom and when these prophecies would come to pass. They asked, "What will be the sign of Your coming, and of the end of the age?" (Matthew 24:3). Jesus did not rebuke the disciples for their curiosity. Instead, He gave a long list of signs that would transpire before His visible return to Jerusalem.

Hundreds of years before Christ's appearance, the interest in Messiah's future kingdom was on Daniel's mind after he received the interpretation of a powerful, end-time prophetic vision. In the final chapter of the Book of Daniel, the prophet asks, "How long shall it be to the end of these wonders?" (Daniel 12:6, KJV). Before sealing his prophetic book, he again inquired of the angel giving him the prophetic information, "What shall be the end of these things" (Daniel 12:8)?

Centuries have passed, and 21st century believers are once again studying the words of the Biblical prophets. Many Christians around the world believe we are in the last days, and that we are the generation who will see ancient prophecies related to the return of Jesus Christ fulfilled!

UNLOCKING THE SCROLLS

As the prophet Daniel wrote the final chapter of his book, he was told that his words were closed up until the time of the end, many would run to and fro and knowledge would be increased (Daniel 12:4). This prediction of increased knowledge alludes not only to human capability and inventions, but also indicates an increase in spiritual understanding. Certainly, this describes our generation. We are the first generation in history that is now able to fully understand how many of the complex prophecies of the Bible can come to pass. Predictions once clouded with mystery are now made clear by the fresh wind of the Holy Spirit, who brings inspiration and illumination to the Scriptures (2 Timothy 3:16; 2 Peter 1:21).

For example, we are told that, at Christ's second coming, "Every eye shall see him" (Revelation 1:7). The concept of every person on earth visibly seeing Christ return was impossible, until the invention of satellites that can instantly transmit information all over the world.

Another passage alludes to men receiving a mark on their foreheads or right hands, and the universal control of buying and selling (Revelation 13:16, 17). Before computers, smart cards and identity chips, this prediction was considered irrelevant. Scholars during the 17th and 18th centuries often wrote they were uncertain how this could happen. In our generation, people can receive a series of numbers that will track them in any nation of the world. You are recognized more often by your numbers than by your name!

A third example is Revelation 17 and 18. The prophet John saw a major city eradicated in one hour (Revelation 18:8, 10, 17 and 19). This would have been unheard of in John's day (A.D. 95), because most cities were constructed of stone. Even if a fire devoured a city, it would burn for several days. However, with the invention of nuclear weapons, any city in the world can be destroyed in an hour, thus producing a tormenting, radioactive smoke (Revelation 18:8-10). These brief examples reveal how knowledge and understanding of prophetic truth has increased in our generation and how the sealed mysteries of the Bible are being unlocked for our understanding!

In our search for prophetic truth, let us go back to the very beginning of the first known prophecy. For years, I assumed the world's first prophecy that was given through a man was the prophecy given to Enoch, and recorded in Jude 14. This was the first major Biblical prophecy from a true prophet, and it predicts the return of the Lord with tens of thousands of His saints!

However, the first recorded prophecy in human history was not that given to Enoch. According to the historian Josephus, God gave a special revelation of the earth's future judgments to the first man, Adam. This is where our research will begin—in the beginning.

CHAPTER 1

THE PROPHECY OF ADAM

The first prediction of humanity's future. . . .

For whatever things were written be-

fore were written for our learning, that

we through the patience and com-

fort of the Scriptures might have hope.

Now may the God of patience and

comfort grant you to be like-minded

toward one another, according to

Christ Jesus, that you may with one

mind and one mouth glorify the God

and Father of our Lord Jesus Christ

(Romans 15:4-6).

Most scholars believe that Enoch, the seventh man born from Adam through Seth's linage, is history's first prophet. The Book of Jude documents Enoch's ancient prophecy, revealing that the Lord would return to earth with tens of thousands of His saints, to execute judgment on unbelievers (Jude 14, 15). Jewish history indicates, however, that a unique prediction of the future was given to the very first man, *Adam.*

Flavius Josephus, the Jewish historian, recorded the account of Adam's prediction. Josephus lived in the first century and wrote a major historical volume called *The Antiquities of the Jews.* His detailed historic record begins with the account of Creation and carries the reader from the Garden of Eden to the destruction of the Temple in the year A.D. 70. Josephus was an eyewitness to the Roman invasion of Jerusalem and the desecration of the Holy Temple, and recorded these sad events in his times.

Josephus revealed that God imparted to Adam a revelation that the earth would be destroyed twice—once by a volume of water and later by the violence of fire. According to him, Adam related this information to his son, Seth, who in turn passed the urgent warning on to *his* sons. This revelation was considered so important that Seth's sons recorded the message in brick and stone. Josephus wrote of the sons of Seth:

> They also were the inventors of that peculiar sort of wisdom which is concerned with the heavenly bodies, and their order. And that their inventions might not be lost before they were sufficiently known, upon Adam's prediction that the world was to be destroyed at one time by the force of fire, and at another time by the violence and quantity of water, they made two pillars, one of brick and the other of stone: they inscribed their discoveries on

them both, that in case the brick might be destroyed by the flood, the pillar of stone might remain, and exhibit these discoveries to mankind; and also to inform them that there was another pillar of brick erected by them. Now this remains in the land of Siriad to this day. (Flavius Josephus, *Antiquities of the Jews*, Chapter II, section 3).

According to the *Book of Jasher,* a historic writing containing early Biblical history, the author gives additional insight to the ancient tablets that contain Adam's written warning. This ancient book is quoted three times in the Old Testament: in Joshua 10:13 and 2 Samuel 1:18, and in 1 Kings 8:53 in the Septuagint translation.

According to the ancient author, Cainan, Seth's grandson engraved these solemn warnings:

And Cainan knew by his wisdom that God would destroy the sons of men for having sinned upon the earth, and that the Lord would in the latter days bring upon them the waters of the flood. And in those days Cainan wrote upon tablets of stone, what was to take place in time to come, and to put them in his treasures (Jasher 2:12, 13).

The reason given for engraving two monuments, one of brick and another of stone, was that if one was destroyed by water, the other would survive. Over 1,900 years ago, Josephus informed his readers that in his day, one of the monuments inscribed with this revelation existed in the land of Siriad, which some scholars believe was located in Egypt. This first warning given to Adam's descendants was passed on in verbal and written form on brick and stone.

THE GENERATIONS OF ADAM

Genesis 5 contains a register of the first 10 generations from Adam to Noah. This register tells us how long each man lived. Translated into English, the Hebrew meaning of the names of these men gives a prophetic picture of future redemption.

English Name	General Hebrew Meaning
1. Adam, v. 3	Man
2. Seth, v. 6	Appointed
3. Enos, v. 9	Mortal
4. Cainan, v. 12	Sorrow
5. Mahalaleel, v. 15	Blessed God
6. Jared, v. 18	Shall Come Down
7. Enoch, v. 21	Teaching
8. Methuselah, v. 25	His Death Brings
9. Lamech, v. 28	Despairing
10. Noah, v. 32	Rest

It appears the Holy Spirit hid a significant message that denotes the future redemption of mankind in the first 10 names of the genealogy from Adam to Noah!

Read these names straight down. Arrange the meanings into one complete statement, and a wonderful, prophetic picture emerges:

Man (is)

Appointed

Mortal

Sorrow; (the)

Blessed God

Shall Come Down

Teaching;

His Death Brings (the)

Despairing

Rest!

The Messiah was a man of sorrow and acquainted with grief (Isaiah 53:3). He came to earth to teach mankind about God's truth. His death and resurrection brought eternal rest to those who believe in Him! Not only is there a message in the meaning of the names, but also each man lived a long life before the time of the flood.

The Man	*Years Lived*
◆ Adam	930 years, Genesis 5:5
◆ Seth	912 years, v. 8
◆ Enos	905 years, v. 11
◆ Cainan	910 years, v. 14
◆ Mahalaleel	895 years, v. 17
◆ Jared	962 years, v. 20
◆ Enoch	365 years, v. 23
◆ Methuselah	969 years, v. 27
◆ Lamech	777 years, v. 31
◆ Noah	950 years, 9:29

[handwritten margin note: Adam Still lived]

These men probably lived in close proximity to each other before the flood. In fact, Adam was still living during the 243rd year of Methuselah's life. So both Adam and Seth could have continually informed their children, grandchildren and great grandchildren about this startling warning from God. It was the seventh generation from Adam, however, that began making preparations for a major cataclysmic event that would soon come.

ENOCH, THE SEVENTH GENERATION

Enoch is listed as the seventh righteous man in Adam's lineage. The Bible gives us unique insight into this early prophet:

> Enoch lived sixty-five years, and begot Methuselah. After he
> begot Methuselah, Enoch walked with God three hundred years,
> and had sons and daughters. So all the days of Enoch were
> three hundred and sixty-five years. And Enoch walked with God;
> and he was not, for God took him (Genesis 5:21-24).

Notice that Enoch began walking with God at age 65, after the birth of Methuselah. Why did the birth of Enoch's son, Methuselah, motivate Enoch toward such spiritual dedication? The meaning of Methuselah's name may shed some light on this question.

The Hebrew name is a combination of the word *met*, which means death, and the word *shelach*, which means to initiate something. The root word means "to throw a spear or a javelin." The English letter *u* in Methuselah's name is the Hebrew letter *vav*, which means *his death*. Therefore, the meaning of Methuselah's name is "his death will initiate," or "his death will bring it."

Apparently, it was revealed to Enoch that something cataclysmic would happen upon the death of Methuselah. Some traditions indicate that Enoch was taken to heaven at age 65, where he received the knowledge of heavenly mysteries. One such revelation was that when his son died, a flood would engulf the earth. Perhaps this is why Enoch began walking with God *after* Methuselah was born (Genesis 5:22).

A Strange New Message

The warning that a large volume of water would cover the earth was a new teaching to those living before the flood. I say this because before Noah's time, no flood of water had ever covered the earth. This is indicated in the Genesis account that describes the creation of the Garden of Eden.

According to Moses, there was one main river that flowed through Eden to provide water for the garden, and it parted into four main branches. These four branches were the Pison, the Gihon, the Euphrates, and the Hiddekel, known today as the Tigris River (Genesis 2:10-14).

The Bible also states that "a mist went up from the earth and watered the whole face of the ground" (Genesis 2:6). Some Christian scientists and researchers believe there was a large firmament, or a canopy similar to the skin on an apple, that once covered the earth. This would mean that the vegetation was watered from the rivers and from the massive, watery vapor (mist) hovering above the ground.

While some scholars offer a different opinion, I believe the prediction of a coming flood of water was a new message, and was not received by the skeptics—especially those from the lineage of Cain. It is hard for people to believe in something they cannot see. It is easy to be fearful of something that has never happened. How could people be fearful of a coming tornado if they have never seen one's path of devastation or experienced its destructive power?

THE THREE LEVELS OF WARNINGS

Enoch was translated alive to heaven at age 365 (Genesis 5:23). His son, Methuselah, was 300 years old at the time of his father's departure. At age 187, Methuselah's first son, Lamech, was born (Genesis 5:25). After 182 years, Lamech's wife gave birth to a son named Noah (Genesis 5:28).

Noah was the tenth generation from Adam and was given the heavy burden of preparing a huge ark to preserve his family and the animal kingdom from total destruction. When he reached the ripe old age of 500, Noah's wife gave birth to three sons: Shem, Ham, and Japheth (Genesis 6:10).

Because all his sons were born when Noah was 500 years old, they may have been triplets. God knew that Noah would need extensive manpower to construct the ark; therefore, his three sons apparently were all born at one time! Noah's motivation for building the ark is found in Hebrews 11:

> By faith Noah, being divinely warned of things not yet seen, moved with godly fear, prepared an ark for the saving of his household, by which he condemned the world and became heir of the righteousness which is according to faith (v. 7).

The fear of earth's future destruction and the opportunity to save his family inspired Noah to spend 100 years in labor—the time needed to build the ark. The most perplexing element of this narrative is that nobody else outside of Noah's immediate family of eight people entered the ark before the flood.

The human population was corrupt and filled with evil imaginations and wicked thoughts (Genesis 6:5). Yet, how could people be so spiritually blind and hardened by sin that they totally disregarded the visible and verbal warnings of impending trouble? In fact, they ignored three obvious warnings that something was about to transpire that would impact the world.

1. Warning Number One: the Predictions of Adam

For over 1,300 years, the warning that the world would be destroyed by water circulated through the descendants of Adam. This oral tradition was no doubt forgotten or ignored as time progressed. Just like today, people soon forget the danger signs when everything is going so well.

The terror and danger of September 11th, 2001, has basically been forgotten, as people have moved on with their lives. Warnings often mean nothing until after the fact.

The global condition in Noah's day reflected a time of prosperity and festivity. People were "eating, drinking, marrying and giving in marriage, until the day Noah entered the ark and God shut the door" (Matthew 24:38). Extreme prosperity may have given the people a false impression of security. Busy people often forget to discern the times because they are too busy just being busy!

2. Warning Number Two: the Record in Stone and Brick

According to Josephus, the prediction of Adam was carved in brick and stone. This was a constant reminder to the future. Every time a person passed by these monuments, written by Seth's sons, they were reminded of information from a righteous man that humanity's wickedness would, in the future, incur the wrath of God. Eventually, the muddy waters of the deluge would engulf the very stones that silently brought the divine warnings!

3. Warning Number Three: the Testimony of Methuselah

The meaning of the name *Methuselah* indicated that his death would initiate a drastic change on earth. Every time a neighbor or friend of the family greeted Methuselah, they understood the meaning of his name: "His death will initiate it." This was another sign that something powerful would transpire on earth at the time of Methuselah's death.

The general population ignored these signs: the oral prophecy of Adam, the records etched in brick and stone, and the name of *Methuselah*. Only eight people heeded, and prepared for the flood. Perhaps as long as Methuselah was living on earth, there was no sense of urgency for people to change their lifestyles and repent. After all, as long as Methuselah was living and walking, nothing bad could happen.

The fact that Methuselah lived 969 years may have added to this false security (Genesis 5:27). Some might have thought the old fellow would never die! However, God permitted him to live an extended life to provide sufficient time for Noah to complete the ark. This phenomenon also pointed to the longsuffering nature of God:

> Who formerly were disobedient, when once the Divine longsuffering waited in the days of Noah, while the ark was being prepared, in which a few, that is, eight souls, were saved through water (1 Peter 3:20).

YET SEVEN MORE DAYS

After more than 100 years, the ark was finished (Genesis 5:32 and 7:6). God spoke to Noah and said, "For after seven more days I will cause it to rain on the earth forty days and forty nights, and I will destroy from the face of the earth all living things" (v. 4).

The ark was completed, the animals were inside, and the door was ready to close. God told Noah He would restrict the flood for seven days. For years, I assumed the Almighty wanted to keep the door open, allowing last minute skeptics an opportunity to repent and run to safety. However, Methuselah died the same year the flood erupted!

In early history, the Hebrews would traditionally mourn seven days after the death of a loved one (Genesis 50:10). In the Law of Moses, if someone touched a dead carcass, he needed seven days to purify himself (Numbers 19:16).

These additional seven days gave Noah time to bury his righteous great-grandfather, Methuselah, and spend seven days in the required purification and mourning. It also enabled him to ensure that all the animals God required were in the ark (Genesis 7:1-4).

After the seven days, the door to the ark was shut tight. The fountains of underground water were released and torrents of rain gushed from the heavenly firmament for 40 consecutive days and nights (Genesis 7:17). At that moment, the terrorized population realized that Adam's prophecy had unexpectedly come to pass, in a day's time! Sadly, it was too late for unbelievers to prepare. The warnings and signs were ignored and all that remained was judgment.

WARNINGS FOR THIS GENERATION

In Noah's day, the warning of a coming flood was a new revelation, and it was ignored by the entire population. The spectacle of an old man and his sons chopping down trees, nailing logs and scraping tar over a floating houseboat for 100 years probably produced a consensus among the people that the old preacher had lost his mind.

Current history is no different. Almighty God is raising up many voices today to proclaim the soon return of His Son, the Lord Jesus Christ. Despite the obvious and accumulating evidence that the time of Jesus' return is near, scoffers still proclaim their unbelief, saying, "Where is the promise of the coming of the Lord?" (2 Peter 3:4). Just as God provided three types of signs in Noah's day that the flood would come, so the same three parallel signs are evident in this generation.

1. THE ORAL PROPHECIES

The Holy Spirit is speaking to the family of God around the world. He is whispering in the spirits of His people that the return of Christ is near. Many cynics, hearing the message, are protesting, "I've heard this theory for years and nothing has happened!"

The fulfillment of a Biblical prophecy is not always an immediate happening. The birth of Christ was 4,000 years after Adam's fall. The Exodus from Egypt was 400 years after Abraham. Adam's prediction was realized 1,300 years after Adam received it.

Prophets predicted both the first and second comings of Christ. If Jesus fulfilled the many promises of His first appearance, and we know He did, He will certainly fulfill the promises of His reappearance. Christ said He would come again and receive us unto Himself (John 14:1-3). In addition to that promise, two angels announced He would return, even as He was ascending:

> And while they looked steadfastly toward heaven as He went up, behold, two men stood by them in white apparel, who also said, "Men of Galilee, why do you stand gazing up into heaven? This same Jesus, who was taken up from you into heaven, will so come in like manner as you saw Him go into heaven" (Acts 1:10, 11).

The two men (angels) who announced that Christ would return again spoke the first prophecy of His return to be recorded only seconds after Christ's Ascension. The Holy Spirit wanted to tell the disciples that Jesus would one day return to the earth at the same location. From that moment on, the second coming of the Messiah became a central theme and doctrine in the first-century church.

2. The Written Word

In Noah's day, the warnings were etched on brick and stone. Today, we have 66 books in the English translation of the Holy Bible that disclose God's outline of redemption and the future Messianic kingdom. The New Testament alone contains about 318 references to Christ's return!

The 10 generations after Adam had a record in brick and stone, but they had no major written revelation of God's word. After 6,000 years of human history, we are blessed to have a complete revelation from God in the Holy Bible. All world religions have their holy books. The Muslims have the Koran and the Buddhists have the traditions of Buddha, but only the inspired Scriptures, penned by prophets and apostles, contain thousands of prophecies that have been or will be fulfilled. This is why the Apostle John wrote, "The testimony of Jesus is the spirit of prophecy" (Revelation 19:10).

The Holy Bible, the written Word of God, reveals God's plans for mankind's future. Those plans include a final world empire controlled by a military dictator identified as the Antichrist. The Apocalypse indicates that a false prophet will unite the world under a false religion (Revelation 13:1-18). The world will be thrust into the great Tribulation (Matthew 24:21). This terrible time will climax with the return of Jesus and the armies of heaven (Revelation 20:1-4). At that moment, the 1,000-year reign of Christ will begin (Revelation 20:1-4).

With these obvious signs being fulfilled in Israel, many among the Gentile nations and in the church are unaware of the warnings and blessings predicted for the future. Part of the overall plan will include a future resurrection of the dead in Christ and a catching away of those who are living on earth, called the Rapture. (More details about this topic are in the next chapter titled "The Enoch Factor.")

3. THE SPOKEN WORD

The third warning comes through the spoken word, the personal testimonies of believers. When Methuselah's name was spoken, the meaning indicated something would happen. Today, thousands of "Methuselahs" preach an urgent message of hope to the believers and a warning to the generation of unbelievers who are ignoring the signs before them. God always sends a messenger before times of great danger, or before seasons of major fulfillment of prophecy.

Joseph preceded the Hebrews to Egypt, Moses preceded the Exodus, Joshua preceded the capture of the Promised Land, and John the Baptist preceded Christ's ministry. Two witnesses will appear in Jerusalem before Christ returns to rule on earth (Revelation 11:1-8). Every messenger came, or is coming, with a warning to the world.

Joseph warned of a coming famine, Moses warned Pharaoh of God's judgments on Egypt, and John the Baptist warned that Jesus would "purge the harvest floor" (Matthew 3:12). The two witnesses will announce God's future judgments and prepare the way for the return of Christ to rule on earth. Prophets and prophecies always precede dramatic, earth-changing prophetic events. Every minister who proclaims the return of Christ is another Noah, or another Methuselah, to his or her generation.

We must have the boldness of Elijah and demand from our generation, "How long will you be divided between two opinions?" (1 Kings 18:21). If the Lord is returning soon, then shout it from the housetops! Those who choose to remain stagnant in their quagmire of unbelief should be warned of the consequences of their choices.

THE SECOND HALF OF ADAM'S WARNING

The first part of the ancient warning given to Adam was fulfilled at the time of Noah's global flood. The second part of Adam's warning predicted the world would be engulfed in fire. This same type of warning is predicted in the New Testament epistles of Peter:

> But the heavens and the earth which are now preserved by the same word, are reserved for fire until the Day of Judgment and perdition of ungodly men (2 Peter 3:7).

I believe this second phase of Adam's warning has been pre-written in numerous passages in both the Old and New Testaments. It is possible that the future great tribulation, which was predicted by the prophets, apostles, and Jesus Christ, will fulfill part of Adam's revelation as weapons of mass destruction will be unleashed upon parts of the earth.

The other aspect of this ancient prophecy may occur at the conclusion of the one thousand year reign of Christ, prior to the formation of a "new heaven and a new earth" (Revelation 21:1, 2).

Let us examine several unusual passages of ancient scriptures that may actually allude to weapons of mass destruction being used in the future, thus fulfilling many of the strange prophecies recorded by the Biblical prophets.

CHAPTER 2

THE WMD FACTOR & CHRIST'S RETURN

Biblical evidence of weapons of mass destruction

The kings of the earth who committed fornication and lived luxuriously with her will weep and lament for her, when they see the smoke of her burning, standing at a distance for fear of her torment, saying, "Alas, alas, that great city Babylon, that mighty city! For in one hour your judgment has come" (Revelation 18:9, 10).

*C*hrist's return to earth will rescue the remaining Jewish remnant living in Israel, and according to John's vision in Revelation chapter eleven, Christ's return will also interrupt the decimation of the earth by men who are instigating war and upheaval. Revelation 11:18 says:

> The nations were angry, and Your wrath has come, and the time of the dead, that they should be judged, and that You should reward Your servants the prophets and the saints, and those who fear Your name, small and great, and should destroy those who destroy the earth.

In the future, the earth will experience an extended season of war, famine and pestilence unlike any time in global history. This seven-year time frame, identified by scholars as the Tribulation, will bring to a climax numerous Biblical prophecies dealing with the last days, the time of the end and the latter days (2 Timothy 3:1-4; Daniel 10:14; 12:4-9).

Scripture indicates that large-scale wars will strike the nations, bringing unimaginable heartache and death to millions of people (Revelation 6:8). The hostilities and destruction that follow will be so dramatic that men will seek sanctuary in caves, and even desire to die (Revelation 6:16; Revelation 9:6).

Centuries ago, scholars and students of Scripture read diverse prophetic passages alluding to gruesome wars and destruction, often questioning how these events could possibly befall the world. Until the invention of modern weapons, battles were fought on horseback, with spears and swords, and, eventually, with guns and bullets. At the present time, with the invention of nuclear, biological, and chemical weapons of mass destruction (abbreviated as WMD), the chilling scenarios seen in the visions of the prophets are possible.

The Big Bomb

During World War II, the nations of the world were stunned with fear when America pulled the atomic bomb out of its secret arsenal. Within one hour, Japan had experienced a weapon so deadly and dangerous that only years later did we realize the hazard that the radioactive fallout had created. Thus began the modern age of weapons of mass destruction.

Years after introducing the nuclear bomb, classified information was stolen, illegally purchased or secretly researched by scientists in third world nations. Their theory was that any nation who could produce nuclear weapons could effectively restrain an invasion from opposing nations. Fifty years later, Great Britain, Russia, China, Israel, North Korea, India, Pakistan, and certain third world countries have their own nuclear capabilities, and are feverishly working in secret laboratories to develop their own stash of nuclear, chemical, and biological weapons.

A leading Islamic imam recently announced the necessity for every Muslim country to begin developing nuclear weapons. This would give them the edge in any future conflict and would also keep America, Israel and Great Britain (the "infidels") from invading Islamic countries and removing the regimes. Intelligence sources indicate that the greatest danger to the future security of the free world is the possibility that Islamic fanatics will soon have these weapons in their possession. At the time of this writing, Iran, one of the most fanatical regimes in the region, is poised to develop nuclear capabilities.

Another danger is that egotistical, self-proclaimed dictators, whose appetite for authority is fed by amassing huge caches of weapons, dominate many third world countries.

Saddam Hussein was such an example. The more nations that obtain a personal warehouse of deadly arms, the more dangerous the world will become.

THE HORSEMEN OF WAR

According to the Bible, during the first half of the future tribulation, various wars and internal clashes will engulf the earth. These apocalyptic conflicts are alluded to in Revelation chapter six, where John saw four horsemen, identified by scholars as the four horsemen of the Apocalypse.

> And I looked, and behold, a white horse. He who sat on it had a bow; and a crown was given to him, and he went out conquering and to conquer. When He opened the second seal, I heard the second living creature saying, "Come and see." Another horse, fiery red, went out. And it was granted to the one who sat on it to take peace from the earth, and that people should kill one another; and there was given to him a great sword.
>
> When He opened the third seal, I heard the third living creature say, "Come and see." So I looked, and behold, a black horse, and he who sat on it had a pair of Scales in his hand. And I heard a voice in the midst of the four living creatures saying, "A quart of wheat for a denarius, and three quarts of barley for a denarius; and do not harm the oil and the wine."
>
> When He opened the fourth seal, I heard the voice of the fourth living creature saying, "Come and see." So I looked, and behold, a pale horse. And the name of him who sat on it was Death, and Hades followed with him. And power was given to them over a fourth of the earth, to kill with sword, with hunger, with death, and by the beasts of the earth (Revelation 6:2-8).

The rider on the white horse was given a crown and a bow to go forth and conquer. Obviously, he is conquering land or territory because the crown represents governmental

leadership and control. In ancient times, the bow represented a military person, so this rider will conquer various
regions of the world through military might. In ancient times,
a bow was kept in a case of leather or cloth. If the bow was
exposed, it signified a preparation for war. The rider has a
bow, signifying the preparation for battle and conquering
through conflict.

Immediately, a red horse followed the white horse, taking peace from the earth. This picture depicts anarchy, as
people turn against one another with a sword. The Old
Testament word for *sword* is used 393 times; and usually
alludes to a war, a conflict or judgment. Another time a
sword was mentioned in the Bible was when Isaac prophesied over his son, Esau:

> By your sword you shall live, and you shall serve your brother;
> and it shall come to pass when you become restless, that you
> shall break his yoke from your neck (Genesis 27:40).

The children who came from Esau settled on Mount Seir
in Jordan and were called Edom (Genesis 36:1). Later, as
they grew into a mighty nation, they were called the
Edomites (Genesis 36:43).

Research indicates that many present-day Palestinians
who live in the West Bank and Gaza strip in Israel are
descendants of the Edomites, who trace their family linage
through Esau. Throughout history, the descendents of Esau
who live in the Promised Land have warred and fought
against the Hebrew people, just as Isaac predicted they
would.

THE GREAT SWORD

Revelation 6:4 speaks of a great sword. The Greek word
great is *megas* and refers to the largest sword used in the

Roman period. In the New Testament, the common Greek word for "kill" is *apokteino*, meaning to kill or destroy. The Greek word used for "kill" in Revelation 6:4 is *sphazo*, and is found only in this place in the New Testament. It means "to butcher and to slaughter, like an animal for a sacrifice." This is not killing through a conventional form of war, but an outright violent slaughter of other people. It appears that when peace is dislodged, a period of complete global anarchy will prevail.

One example of this meaning is the account of two Islamic Imams who met in Iraq after the the second Iraqi war for the purpose of reconciliation. When the people came together, a mob rose up with knives and swords, and butchered a noted Islamic religious leader. This action shocked the world, because Muslims killed their own religious leader with swords.

Some have suggested this future anarchy prophesied may occur because of the confusion caused by the sudden removal of millions through the Rapture, the "catching away" of the church (1 Thessalonians 4:16, 17). This theory is possible, but it is only speculation, because the Bible does not indicate such.

The third horse and rider introduce a major famine on the earth. Wheat and barley, both used to make bread, will be rationed at a high price. The price of a quart of wheat costs a whole day's wages.

Again, this scenario was more recently demonstrated during the war in Iraq. A major military conflict always disrupts the roads, airports, ports, electricity, and all forms of communication. Food rationing may occur not because no food is being grown, but because the human slaughter and multiple military conflicts create a disastrous humanitarian crisis.

We also learn in Revelation 11:6 that it will not rain for 42 months. This ecologic disruption would create the conditions for a food shortage and famine.

The fourth horse, identified as pale, initiates a combination of sword (war), hunger (famine) and death. Two of the four horsemen carry a sword, indicating that the Tribulation will be a period of violent military clashes, war, and civil conflict as the nations on earth are thrust into sudden chaos and confusion.

In my book *Unleashing the Beast*, I explain the Islamic traditions about the future rise of the Mahdi, an Islamic leader anticipated by Muslims around the world. Muslims believe he will introduce Islamic justice and peace to the entire world. This peace will depend, however, on people accepting the Koran, Islam's holy book, and Mohammad as the final prophet and messenger of God (Allah). Those who resist the Mahdi's form of justice will be met with swift punishment through the "sword of Islam."

Perhaps this is why the Bible indicates that people who do not follow the final tyrant will be beheaded during the Tribulation (Revelation 20:4). Islamic radicals and strict Islamic governments still use the sword to slice off the right hand of a thief and behead those who have committed high crimes. This form of punishment has been witnessed first hand in countries where fanatical Islamic militants have slaughtered Christians.

At the present time, many of the Muslim nations are making a great effort to obtain weapons of mass destruction. Small, self-proclaimed terrorist groups, such as Islamic Jihad, Al Qaeda, Hamas, and countless others are making determined efforts to acquire deadly biological and chemical agents that could decimate the population in a major city.

MODERN WEAPONS SEEN BY THE PROPHETS

In Revelation 6, Jesus Christ opens a sealed book in heaven just as the Tribulation begins on earth. As he opens the sixth seal:

> I looked when He opened the sixth seal, and behold, there was a great earthquake; and the sun became black as sackcloth of hair, and the moon became like blood. And the stars of heaven fell to the earth, as a fig tree drops its late figs when it is shaken by a mighty wind. Then the sky receded as a scroll when it is rolled up, and every mountain and island was moved out of its place (Revelation 6:12-14).

When this seal is opened, severe cosmic disturbances follow. The sun will turn black in the sky, and the moon will take on the color of blood. Many Jewish rabbis believe this sackcloth sun alludes to a complete solar eclipse, and the blood moon refers to a lunar eclipse with the moon taking on a reddish-orange color. Another interpretation is that this scenario may be painting the imagery of a nuclear winter.

A great earthquake occurs at the same time of the cosmic activity (Revelation 6:12). The Greek word for earthquake is *seismos*, which can mean a local earthquake or a strong shaking of the earth. The ancient prophet predicted that one day the earth would be shaken out of its place (Isaiah 13:13), and that it would "reel to and fro like a drunk man" (Isaiah 24:20). Any massive nuclear bomb causes the area within miles to shake violently, producing an atomic earthquake.

Scientists say that during a thermonuclear war, a nuclear blast would affect the atmosphere by blotting out a portion of light and heat from the sun.

The verse that catches the attention of the informed student of prophecy is when "the sky receded as a scroll when it is rolled up" (Revelation 6:14). A thermonuclear blast creates a giant vacuum of air that is pushed out and then folds inward upon itself. To a first century man who sees a nuclear explosion in a vision, it would appear that the sky is folding in on itself, similar to the way an ancient scroll is rolled open from two sides and closed again from both ends.

A massive nuclear explosion would cause the mountains and islands to be moved out of their places, as John indicated in his vision (Revelation 6:14). With this scenario before him, no wonder John spoke of one-third of mankind being killed by fire, smoke and brimstone (Revelation 9:18). Modern weapons of mass destruction could easily cause the massive number of deaths alluded to in the Book of Revelation!

DESTRUCTION IN ONE HOUR

In John's time, buildings in major cities such as Jerusalem and Rome were constructed of quarried stone and marble. Among the ruins of the former Roman Empire, one can see today the giant marble columns, the huge stone walls, and the quarried limestone used for public buildings, sports coliseums and amphitheaters.

In the first century, it would have taken quite a long time to completely burn an entire city the size of Rome. In fact, during the time of the apostle Paul, a wicked emperor named Nero ruled the Roman Empire. His selfish desire was to tear down much of Rome, and rebuild it to place a statue of himself in the center of every building. When the Roman Senate refused his request, Nero set Rome on fire, afterwards blaming the tragedy on Christians! Nero sent his servants to every quarter, setting the city in a blaze.

According to some accounts, Rome burned for more than a month and only one of the 12 sections of the city survived the blaze!

The interior of the buildings consisted of fabrics, wood, and furniture that could catch fire quickly, but many ruins of the weather-worn stone structures, marble columns, and bits of stone walls still exist as tourist monuments to this day. Ancient Rome burned for weeks but, in the future, the city will be destroyed in one hour!

MYSTERY BABYLON DESTROYED

The apostle John indicates a tragic event will transpire toward the conclusion of the great Tribulation. A major global city will be wiped out in an hour's time. The city marked for destruction is cryptically identified as "Mystery Babylon." In Revelation 17, John describes it as the city "ruling over the kings of the earth," and the city "drunken with the blood of the saints and the blood of the martyrs of Jesus" (Revelation 17:6). The city ruling over kings in John's day and the city responsible for persecuting and murdering early Christians was the city of Rome, Italy.

Some ask, "Why didn't John just come out and identify the city as Rome? Why did he cryptically veil the identification of the city?" John received the vision of the Book of Revelation on the Island of Patmos (Revelation 1:9) while he was a Roman political prisoner.

If John had clearly written that Rome would one day be destroyed, the Book of Revelation would have never been permitted to leave the island! The scroll would have been considered an anti-Roman government manuscript and would have been confiscated by Roman authorities and destroyed.

When John described dragons in the sky (Revelation 12), a woman travailing in heaven (Revelation 12), and beasts rising out of the sea (Revelation 13:1-11), the Roman guards on the island may have said, "This old man (John) claimed to see a vision. He must have been drinking at the time! Let him keep his old scroll." John actually hid the true identity of mystery Babylon, I believe, for security reasons and to protect those who would read the vision in the local churches.

Note that in Jewish sources also, Babylon was a symbol for Rome. The *Greek Apocalypse of Ezra* (*4 Ezra* and *2 Ezra 3, 4*), the *Syriac Apocalypse of Baruch* (*2 Apocalypse of Baruch*), and the *Sibylline Oracles* all compare Rome to Babylon. So identifying John's mysterious city as Rome agrees with other historical comparisons of that day.

Since the inception of the Roman Empire, Rome has been a major city, first politically and then spiritually. Politically, it was the capital of the Roman Empire and was dominated by Caesars who used Rome's military strength to occupy the known world before and after the birth of Christ. After Constantine the Great became the first Christian Emperor of the Roman Empire, the Empire mixed politics and religion together, forming the first empire to be controlled and molded by religion.

In the eleventh century, this system divided between the west (Roman Christianity) and the east (Orthodox Christianity). The Roman branch (Roman Catholicism) remained the dominant branch.

Since 1929, the Vatican has been a country within itself and has been directly involved with negotiations between Israel and the Palestinians. The Pope has made commendable statements toward the Muslims, and the Vatican, along with the city of Rome, has given permission for one of the largest mosques in Europe to be built in Rome. While the friendship between the Roman church and the Muslims is warm, in the future the city of Rome will be destroyed in one hour.

> Standing at a distance for fear of her torment, saying, "Alas, alas, that great city Babylon, that mighty city! For in one hour your judgment has come" (Revelation 18:10).

For in one hour such great riches came to nothing. Every shipmaster, all who travel by ship, sailors, and as many as trade on the sea, stood at a distance and cried out when they saw the smoke of her burning, saying, "What is like this great city . . . for in one hour she is made desolate" (Revelation 18:17-19).

DEADLY EXPLOSION IN ROME

Not only will a massive nuclear explosion wipe out the city in a single hour, but the radioactive fallout from the massive radiation cloud will cause great fear for everyone living in the surrounding area. This fearful reaction may be alluded to in the verse that says that people are weeping and standing afar off for fear because of the torment and the smoke (Revelation 18:9, 10). In one hour, the city will be decimated; and in one day, the city suffers death, mourning and famine because it was burned with fire (Revelation 18:8).

If this is a correct interpretation of future events, then the final eighth kingdom of prophecy will literally be an Islamic-controlled empire. The reasoning behind the destruction of Rome would be to physically remove any trace of traditional Christianity from the earth. There are many Christian churches with international headquarters located in cities throughout the world, but no city is recognized as the mother of historic Roman Christianity as is Rome.

In the Middle East, the Islamic world does not recognize the world headquarters of any modern Protestant denomination, but through the centuries has always been linked to the priests of the Roman church system. This is because in much of the Middle East, the Roman and the Orthodox churches have thousands of buildings, along with orphanages and, in some areas, Christian schools. The Roman system existed before the founding of the Islamic religion in the seventh century.

Islam and Roman Christianity have occasionally locked horns and, from the 11th to the 14th centuries, have fought wars in Europe and the Middle East. The goal of the final Antichrist and his global religion will be to set himself up as God and remove any visage of religion other than his own. Leading the charge of this transformation will be a man identified in prophecy as the false prophet (Revelation 13:11-18). The future Antichrist will rule from Jerusalem's Temple Mount and the false prophet will make an image for humanity to worship. The epicenter of this new global religion will not be Mecca (for Islam), or Rome (for Roman Catholics), but Jerusalem, Israel - the place holy to Jews, Christians, and Muslims!

The destruction of Rome will be a prelude to massive warfare and destruction, eventually climaxing in the mother of all battles, identified by scholars as the famous Battle of Armageddon (Revelation 16:16).

THE WAR OF GOG AND MAGOG

One of the dominant battles of Biblical prophecy will unfold in the distant future. Scholars identify this conflict as the War of Gog and Magog. The prophet Ezekiel saw this prophetic conflict over 2,600 years ago! Not only do Evangelical Christians believe this major war will actually occur, but Jewish rabbis living in Israel also acknowledge this prophecy as a future event.

Notably, the Islamic religion has also developed a tradition about the future war of Gog and Magog. All three monotheistic religions whose roots are in Abraham—Christianity, Judaism, and Islam—acknowledge the truth of this prophecy in Ezekiel 38 and 39 in some form or other. Modern scholars have also called this battle, World War III.

This deadly clash of nations will occur on the mountains north and east of modern Israel. One location of heavy fighting is identified as Bashan, presently the Golan Heights area (Ezekiel 39:18). The modern Bashan area was once possessed by Syria and was seized by Israel in the 1967 war.

The other sector specified in the prophecy is the Valley of the Passengers to the east of the sea (Ezekiel 39:11). In the Hebrew text, the Valley of the Passengers is the Abarim Mountains, nestled on the east side of the Jordan River. It is presently located in the country of Jordan. I have stood near these very mountains, which surround Mount Nebo, the site where Moses caught his final view of the Promised Land before his death (Deuteronomy 32:49).

In his vision, the prophet Ezekiel lists the coalition of nations involved in this attempted siege of Israel. It is interesting that the participating players listed are currently strong Islamic nations, except for the foremost nation directing the assault, which will be a Russian coalition. This will, no doubt, consist of the five southern Russian states that were once a part of the ancient Turkish Empire. The Gog/Magog battle will include:

1. Libya (Ezekiel 38:5)
2. Ethiopia (Ezekiel 38:5)
3. Persia—present-day Iran (Ezekiel 38:5)
4. Togarmah—present-day Turkey (Ezekiel 38:6)
5. Gomer—present-day Germany (Ezekiel 38:6)
6. Meshech and Tubal—present-day Russia (Ezekiel 38:3)

As the battle is launched, hordes of invading armies will swarm onto the mountains of northern Israel and the land east of the Jordan River. The battle will become so fierce that five-sixths of the Islamic hordes will be decimated on the mountains of Israel. The enormous number of weapons will require seven years for men to clean out the land (Ezekiel 39:9).

The most intriguing part of the prophecy is:

> "For seven months the house of Israel will be burying them, in order to cleanse the land. Indeed all the people of the land will be burying, and they will gain renown for it on the day that I am glorified," says the Lord God. "They will set apart men regularly employed, with the help of a search party, to pass through the land and bury those bodies remaining on the ground, in order to cleanse it. At the end of seven months they will make a search. The search party will pass through the land; and when anyone sees a man's bone, he will set up a marker by it, till the buriers have buried it in the Valley of Hamon Gog. The name of the city will also be Hamonah. Thus they shall cleanse the land" (Ezekiel 39:12-16).

The burial process for those killed in this battle is very strange. Normally, in warfare the corpses of those slain in battle are amassed immediately after the conflict. In this scenario, foreigners will be hired by the Israelis to scan the ground for bones and charred remnants of dead soldiers. Special signs will be erected at the site of any bones. Later, the physical remains will be buried in a valley that will be named Hamon-gog, meaning "the multitude of Gog"

(Ezekiel 39:11). In the text, the search for corpses will begin seven months after the battle concludes. Why would there be a seven-month delay in searching the battlefield and posting signs near the human remains?

There is speculation, which I believe is correct, that a diversity of weapons of mass destruction will be used in the conflict. The release of certain biological and chemical weapons would defile miles of land, thus making it dangerous for humans to venture into the vicinity of contamination for several months.

WHO HAS THE WEAPONS?

When the United States and its coalition struck Iraq in the 2003 war, a reason given for the invasion was the possibility that Saddam Hussein and his cronies were secretly developing weapons of mass destruction. After the war, the news media began a campaign to discredit the President of the United States and the Prime Minister of Great Britain for misleading their people with false information as an excuse to conduct a war. The information about the existence of these weapons programs came from four sources:

1. Defectors from Iraq who had worked close to the Iraqi administration
2. Intelligence gathered from inside Iraq
3. Intelligence from countries such as Israel
4. Intelligence gathered within the United States from various sources

Where are the weapons that were allegedly being produced? Since the landmass in Iraq is equal to the size of California, there are countless places where vials or tubes of chemicals could be hidden. Some people in Iran believe certain weapons were placed in oil tankers and removed months before the war.

Some intelligence sources inside Israel also believe that some of Iraq's alleged chemical and biological weapons of mass destruction were transported before the war through Syria and into Lebanon. Some Israeli sources indicate they may have been buried in the Bekka Valley, a place noted for pockets of Islamic fanatics. If this is true, then it is possible that the very weapons being hid in this area north of Israel may be a part of the arsenal that will pollute the upper region of Israel in the coming war.

Ezekiel details an environmental backlash in this war. The prophet speaks of the fish in the sea, the birds of heaven, and the beasts of the field being affected by this violent clash of humanity. Ezekiel 38:20 states:

> So that the fish of the sea, the birds of the heavens, the beasts of the field, all creeping things that creep on the earth, and all men who are on the face of the earth shall shake at my presence. The mountains shall be thrown down, the steep places shall fall, and every wall shall fall to the ground.

Ezekiel predicts that the entire creation will "shake at God's presence, and the mountains shall be thrown down and all the steep places shall fall, and every wall shall fall to the ground" (Ezekiel 38:20). As the war rages in the Promised Land, the anointed visionary of God described an "overflowing rain, and great hailstones, fire and brimstone" (Ezekiel 38:22).

RAIN, HAIL, AND BRIMSTONE

Is this rain, hail and brimstone a natural phenomenon? Or is it another indicator of nuclear or biological weapons? Open-air hydrogen bomb tests have resulted in fireballs, dangerous radiation and hailstones. Years ago, when testing the atomic bomb, the military noted that some large ships had thousands of huge dents on their outer armor. It was later revealed that the blast affected the atmosphere and produced huge chunks of ice that fell from the sky, crashing into the ship's monstrous metal frame.

Ezekiel also mentions brimstone. The early Biblical cities of Sodom and Gomorrah were decimated by fire and brimstone showering out of the sky (Genesis 19:24). Modern archaeologists believe a massive volcanic eruption blew the twin cities apart. Evidence of this eruption can be seen to this day at the south of the Dead Sea, in the Jordan area, not far from the suspected location of Sodom and Gomorrah. At the time of the destruction, it would have appeared to Abraham that fire and brimstone were falling from heaven:

> But on the day that Lot went out of Sodom it rained fire and
> brimstone from heaven and destroyed them all. Even so will it be
> in the day when the Son of Man is revealed   (Luke 17:29, 30).

The Golan Heights area was also once an active volcanic region. Large black stones protrude from the ground from the Sea of Galilee throughout the northern part of Israel, all the way to the border of Syria and Lebanon. No volcanic activity has been reported for centuries; therefore, the brimstone that will fall during the Gog and Magog conflict must be something different than a volcanic explosion.

Brimstone is mentioned seven times in the Old Testament prophecies and eight times in the New Testament. Seven of the New Testament references are in the Book of Revelation. The Hebrew meaning of brimstone in the Old Testament is "sulfur." Ezekiel indicates fire and brimstone will fall on the mountains of Israel during the invasion of the northern enemies. One of the chief ingredients in certain chemical agents and nerve gases is sulfur!

Just as fire and brimstone rained upon the wicked cities of Sodom and Gomorrah in Lot's time, another form of fire and brimstone will plague the land before Christ's return. I believe this fire and brimstone could be the product of biological, chemical, and even nuclear weapons used in upcoming warfare. Many other unusual prophecies could allude to weapons of mass destruction being unleashed in the final conflicts.

Modern weapons of mass destruction appear to have been identified thousands of years before they were invented. Other Biblical prophecies also clearly indicate the high-level risk of mass destruction in the future wars of prophecy.

NO FLESH WOULD BE SAVED

Jesus warned about the great Tribulation and indicated that, if the days were not shortened, no flesh would be saved (Matthew 24:22). To illustrate the truth of this, when a small amount of anthrax was mailed through the Postal Service in 2001, the physical and economic impact was unbelievable. That small amount caused several deaths or sickness, and shut down an entire wing of the U.S. Senate office building for several weeks. Imagine the impact one gallon of anthrax would have in a major city or a sports coliseum!

The wars of the future Tribulation could contribute to food shortages, and the injury to the environment could create the food rationing and famines mentioned in Revelation 6:6. These harsh shortages could be the trigger that will usher in a universal brand for buying and selling, identified as the Mark of the Beast. No person will be able to purchase goods or sell products unless they use

the mark, the name, or the number of the beast system
(Revelation 13:11-18). By rationing and controlling the food
supply, the future antichrist system could manipulate
nations and control humanity like a puppet master pull-
ing a puppet's strings.

Isaiah visualized this time and said that men's faces
shall be as flames (Isaiah 13:8). The prophet also pointed
out how these fiery judgments would exterminate throngs
of humanity. He wrote:

> Therefore the curse has devoured the earth, and those who dwell
> in it are desolate. Therefore the inhabitants of the earth are burned,
> and few men are left (Isaiah 24:6).

These words from Isaiah indicate that violent warfare
will destroy large populations of people. This may explain
a rather bizarre prophecy found in Isaiah that reveals the
number of women per men at the conclusion of the tribulation. Isaiah 4:1 states:

> And in that day seven women shall take hold of one man, saying,
> "We will eat our own food and wear our own apparel; only let us
> be called by your name, to take away our reproach."

The ratio of women to men will be seven women for
every one man. Perhaps this will be the result of the large
numbers of men killed during the Tribulation. The Book of
Revelation indicates a fourth of the world's population will
be slain in the early part of the Tribulation by war and
famine (Revelation 6:8).

Later, another one-third of mankind will be killed as
the Tribulation judgments, wars and famines sweep the
earth (Revelation 9:18). Centuries ago, these prophecies
were difficult to interpret. However, with the development
of weapons of mass destruction, these disturbing predictions can become a reality within an hour.

THE SECOND HALF OF ADAM'S PREDICTION REVISITED

The first half of Adam's prediction came to pass when the floodwaters topped the earth. The second half of Adam's prophecy—the destruction of the earth with fire—could occur partially during the seven-year Tribulation. The full prediction will unfold at the conclusion of the 1,000-year reign of Christ. The old heaven and old earth will pass away (Revelation 21:1).

The Greek phrase for passed away is *parerchomai*, and alludes to "changing from one condition to another." God does not obliterate our planet as some pessimistic teachers imagine. Instead, He will take this old earth and renew it into a perfect condition. Most scholars believe this will be accomplished by a renovation with fire:

> Looking for and hastening the coming of the day of God, because of which the heavens will be dissolved, being on fire, and the elements will melt with fervent heat. Nevertheless we, according to his promise, look for new heavens and a new earth, in which righteousness dwells (2 Peter 3:12, 13).

When this process is complete, the second part of Adam's prediction will be complete. At that time, there will be a new heaven and a new earth (Revelation 21:1). All things will be as perfect as they were before Adam sinned. Until then, the parallels of the ten generations from Adam to Noah reveal many of the aspects of future prophetic events.

Another interesting parallel is found in Enoch's translation to heaven. This translation, the first in history, is a picture of the future catching away of the church. Let us examine the story of Enoch and search for the clues that give us a picture of the future catching away and gathering together of the saints to God in heaven.

CHAPTER 3

THE ENOCH FACTOR

A preview of the great catching away

For the Lord Himself will descend from heaven with a shout, with the voice of an archangel, and with the trumpet of God. And the dead in Christ will rise first. Then we who are alive and remain shall be caught up together with them in the clouds to meet the Lord in the air. And thus we shall always be with the Lord. Therefore comfort one another with these words (1 Thessalonians 4:16-18).

O ne of the Bible's most unique and mysterious figures is an early prophet named Enoch. While the Bible devotes three main passages to this seventh descendant from Adam, Jewish apocryphal literature from the second Temple period is filled with rich traditions.

He is said to "have learned God's mysteries and had access to the heavenly tablets." (*Encyclopedia Judaica*, Vol. 6, page 794). Two Jewish apocalyptic books are ascribed to him, and they are known as the *Ethiopic* and the *Slavonic Book of Enoch*. He is mentioned frequently in certain Dead Sea Scrolls, and his story and the writings attested to him are found in the ancient book of *Jubilees*.

A prophecy penned in the New Testament Book of Jude is credited by the writer to have come from Enoch (Jude 14, 15). When we are researching additional information on Enoch, we must examine the various Jewish traditions related to his life. Although this work is not considered inspired as the Holy Scriptures are, it does give us valuable insight into information that was available during the first few centuries of the early church.

The *Ethiopic Book of Enoch*, from the Second Temple period, is divided into five sections. The first (1-36) deals with how fallen angels lusted after the daughters of men and produced a race of wicked giants. The second section (37-71), deals with the "last day," and with the Messiah, who is called the "Elect One."

The third section (72-82), is a rather strange section known as the Book of the Heavenly Luminaries. It gives the mysterious course of the sun, moon and stars. It teaches the "true" calendar is 364 days per year, or 52 weeks. The fourth section (83-90) is similar to section two, and it covers the period of Noah's flood and follows history to the beginning of the Hasmonean period (Greek influence).

The fifth section (91-108), divides history into 10 periods, seven of which have already passed. The last three indicate that the righteous shall triumph, the Temple will be rebuilt and the day of the last judgment will come. The second part (106, 107) deals with Noah's and Enoch's instructions to mankind.

> The Book of Enoch was never included in the canon of Scripture, although some early fathers such as Tertullian, considered the book as part of the Biblical canon. As time passed, contemporary Biblical scholars disseminated the book in the world of western scholarship (*Encyclopedia Judaica*, Vol. 6, page 795).

However interesting these writings may be to a curious student, we must focus our attention on the inspired Biblical narrative for information related to this righteous man, Enoch:

> Enoch lived sixty-five years, and begot Methuselah. After he begot Methuselah, Enoch walked with God three hundred years, and had sons and daughters. So all the days of Enoch were three hundred and sixty-five years. And Enoch walked with God; and he was not, for God took him (Genesis 5:21-24).

> By faith Enoch was taken away so that he did not see death, and was not found, because God had taken him; for before he was taken he had this testimony, that he pleased God (Hebrews 11:5).

> Now Enoch, the seventh from Adam, prophesied about these men also, saying, "Behold, the Lord comes with ten thousands of his saints, to execute judgment on all, to convict all who are ungodly among them of all their ungodly deeds which they have committed in an ungodly way, and of all the harsh things which ungodly sinners have spoken against Him" (Jude 14, 15).

Enoch is the first of two men who were translated alive into heaven, the other being the prophet Elijah (2 Kings 2). There is not much detailed information in the Bible about Enoch's earthly life, but we can collect important parallels about his earthly presence and translation, and how it reveals a wonderful picture of the future translation (Rapture) of the church to heaven! These parallels are discovered when examining three aspects of Enoch's life on earth.

ENOCH PROPHESIED THE COMING OF THE LORD.

According to Jude's account, Enoch was given a vision of the Lord's future return to earth. According to Enoch, the Lord's coming would be accompanied by "ten thousands of His saints" (Jude 14). Over 2,000 years after Enoch, Daniel experienced a vision of heaven in which he described "ten thousand times ten thousand" ministering to the Lord before His throne (Daniel 7:10).

In A.D. 95, the apostle John experienced a vision while he was a prisoner on the Isle of Patmos (Revelation 1:9). He also saw a huge multitude of people standing before God's throne in worship (Revelation 5:11). The visions of Daniel, John and other Hebrew prophets agree with the initial revelation given to Enoch that the Lord will come with a countless multitude of his saints. Three thousand years after Enoch, John painted a complete picture when he wrote:

> Now I saw heaven opened, and behold, a white horse. And He who sat on him was called Faithful and True, and in righteousness He judges and makes war. His eyes were like a flame of fire, and on His head were many crowns. He had a name written that no one knew except Himself. He was clothed with a robe dipped in blood,

and His name is called The Word of God. And the armies in heaven, clothed in fine linen, white and clean, followed Him on white horses. Now out of His mouth goes a sharp sword, that with it He should strike the nations. And He Himself will rule them with a rod of iron. He Himself treads the winepress of the fierceness and wrath of Almighty God. And He has on His robe and on His thigh a name written: KING OF KINGS AND LORD OF LORDS (Revelation 19:11-16).

Many parallels are found when comparing Enoch's prophecy with the Apostle John's predictions in the Book of Revelation, especially chapter 19. This comparison helps to support the authenticity of Enoch's prophecy that is recorded in the New Testament Book of Jude.

Enoch's Vision	John's Vision
The Lord is coming.	The Lord is coming.
The Lord is coming to earth.	He is coming to earth.
He is coming with His saints.	He is coming with His saints.
He will execute judgments.	He will execute judgment.
The ungodly will be judged.	He smites the wicked nations with a rod of iron.

ENOCH WAS THE SEVENTH FROM ADAM.

In Scripture, the number *seven* is an important number mentioned in the Bible 463 times. The number seven is acknowledged as a number indicating completion, and is also considered God's sacred number. It is commonly used when God is emphasizing a pattern for completion, fulfillment, or a spiritual truth.

Enoch, the seventh generation from Adam, experienced a supernatural, bodily translation into heaven. As Enoch was the seventh from Adam, so the number *seven* was important in the creative process of heaven and earth. The Genesis account says God worked six days to complete His creative process. On the seventh day, God rested from His labors (Genesis 2:2).

The Bible teaches that one day with the Lord is as a thousand years and a thousand years as one day (Psalms 90:4). Some scholars as well as early church fathers believed the six days of Creation could allude to the first 6,000 years of human history and government. For example, Irenaeus, born in A.D. 140, wrote a powerful treatise on the Christian faith. He said:

> For in so many days as this world was made, in so many thousand years shall it be concluded . . . and God brought to a conclusion on the sixth day the works He made (Irenaeus, *Against Heresies*. Book V, Chapter 28, Section 3).

The *Epistle of Barnabas*, which dates back to the fourth century, reflects the thoughts of some early theologians. It is written:

> And God made in six days the works of His hands; and He finished them on the seventh day, and He rested on the seventh day, and sanctified it. Consider, my children, what that signifies, He finished them in six days.
>
> The meaning is this: in six thousand years the Lord God will bring all to an end. For with Him one day is a thousand years; as Himself testifieth, saying, behold this day shall be as a thousand years.
>
> Therefore children, in six days, that is in six thousand years, shall all things be accomplished. And what is that He saith and He rested on the seventh day: He meaneth this; that when His son shall come and abolish the season of the wicked one, and shall

change the sun moon and stars, then shall gloriously rest on the seventh day.

A book called *Secrets of Enoch* says that God revealed to Enoch that the world would exist for a total of 7,000 years. This writing dates to the first century A.D. and was translated into the Slavonic language. It reads:

And I appointed the eighth day also that the eighth day should be created after my work, and that the first seven revolve in the form of the seventh thousand, and that at the beginning of the eight thousand there should be a time not counting—endless.

From the first to the fourth centuries, some early theologians debated extensively about the correlation between the six days of Creation in Genesis 1, and the 6,000 years of human government. Since the reign of Christ in Revelation 20:4 is a thousand years, then the 1,000 years could allude to *one prophetic day* in God's sight. And since the millennial reign is a time of rest and peace, it correlates with the seventh day of creation where God rested and ceased His labors.

According to the traditional Christian calendar, from the creation of Adam to the present is slightly over 6,000 years. However, the Jewish calendar counts time from Adam's creation to the year 2004 as 5,764 years. The Jewish calendar remains about 236 years behind the present Christian calendar.

The common explanation for the variation is that God ceased to count prophetic time when Israel was taken into captivity to other nations. One illustration of this would be the time of the Judges and the 70 years in Babylonian captivity. In other words, Hebrew time was not counted when Israel was in captivity or in unbelief as a nation. Based on this theory, God ceased counting time whenever Israel went into captivity.

Another example is found in the Book of Judges. After Israel possessed the Promised Land, they had no king. Scripture says that everyone in the Hebrew nation "did what was right in his own eyes" (Judges 21:25). The Hebrews eventually turned to idolatry, and God permitted their enemies to dominate them through a time of captivity. Judges points this out:

Scripture	Israel's sin	Captivity
Judges 3:8	They did evil	8 years
Judges 3:14	They did evil	18 years
Judges 4:3	They did evil	20 years
Judges 6:1	They did evil	7 years
Judges 10:8	They did evil	18 years
Judges 13:1	They did evil	40 years

Total time in captivity   111 years

Add 70 years of Babylonian captivity and the above total increases from 111 years to 181 years. Also, there were numerous occasions when Israel sinned and their enemies were permitted to overtake them for a season. Some rabbis include other deductions, such as the 13 years when Abraham was raising Ishmael, as a time of unbelief for Israel (Genesis 17:25).

Rabbis explain that this is why the Jewish calendar is short over 236 years from the normal calculated time of Adam to the year 2004. They teach that during the times when Israel was in unbelief or captivity, God stopped counting prophetic time.

Some suggest that this theory of six days and 6,000 years cannot be accurate, since we are already past the 6,000 year mark from Adam. I suggest that it is a laborious task to calculate the exact time using our modern calendars. With the many changes in calendars over the centuries, it is futile to attempt to calculate the exact number of years from Adam to now.

The purpose of this is to show how Enoch's translation occurred in the seventh generation from Adam, not to pinpoint a precise time period. We are presently in the seventh millennium from Adam. Just as Enoch escaped natural death, there is a chosen generation of believers who will experience a glorious translation to heaven at an event known as the "catching away" and the "gathering together!"

> For the Lord Himself will descend from heaven with a shout, with the voice of an archangel, and with the trumpet of God. And the dead in Christ will rise first. Then we who are alive and remain shall be caught up together with them in the clouds to meet the Lord in the air. And thus we shall always be with the Lord (1 Thessalonians 4:16, 17).

> That in the dispensation of the fullness of the times He might gather together in one all things in Christ, both which are in heaven and which are on earth, in Him (Ephesians 1:10).

This "catching up" and "gathering together" is called the Rapture, a theological word used to describe the event where the living saints will be changed in a moment and given a new body, then caught up (literally seized by force) to meet the Lord in the air! Paul spoke of this event when writing to the church at Corinth:

> Behold, I tell you a mystery: We shall not all sleep, but we shall all be changed—in a moment, in the twinkling of an eye, at the last

trumpet. For the trumpet will sound, and the dead will be raised incorruptible, and we shall be changed. For this corruptible must put on incorruption, and this mortal must put on immortality. So when this corruptible has put on incorruption, and this mortal has put on immortality, then shall be brought to pass the saying that is written: "Death is swallowed up in victory" (1 Corinthians 15:51-54).

Enoch's bodily translation to heaven is a beautiful preview of the day when the living saints will be suddenly snatched up into the air to be with the Lord. Then the words of Christ will be fulfilled, which said, "I go to prepare a place for you, and if I go prepare a place for you I will come again and receive you to myself that where I am there you may be also" (John 14:1-3).

Enoch was simply walking with God, minding his own business, when he suddenly vanished from the planet! One day all believers will be simply going about their daily routine, and will suddenly be missing.

ARE WE IN THE EARLY SEVENTH MILLENNIUM?

Because Enoch lived in the seventh generation and was translated, could it be that the return of the Lord will happen in the seventh millennium, which is actually the millennium we are presently in? From the creation of Adam, toward the conclusion of each 1,000-year period, a major event that influenced prophetic movements has occurred:

- The great event of the first millennium was Enoch's translation.
- The great event of the second millennium was the Abrahamic Covenant.
- The great event of the third millennium was David capturing Jerusalem.

♦   The great event of the fourth millennium was the birth of Jesus.

♦   The great event of the fifth millennium was the east/west split of the church.

♦   The great event of the sixth millennium was Israel being restored.

♦   The great event of the seventh millennium could be the rule and reign of Christ.

Enoch was Translated, or Caught Up.

Enoch is one of the two men in Scripture who were translated alive into heaven. Enoch's swift translation into heaven is a perfect picture of the future translation of the church into heaven. This translation is referred to in Ephesians 1:9, 10 as the "gathering together," and in 1 Thessalonians 4:17 as the saints being "caught up together . . . to meet the Lord in the air."

Three men in the Old Testament reveal a picture of future events related to the return of Christ to catch away the believers and resurrect the dead: Enoch, Moses and Elijah.

1. The Translation of Enoch

Enoch was walking with God and was suddenly snatched off the planet (Genesis 5:24). When Christ returns for those whose names are in the Lamb's Book of Life, these saints will be changed from mortal to immortal, in a moment, as fast as the twinkling of an eye (1 Corinthians 15:51).

We will be "caught up . . . to meet the Lord in the air" and we will forever be with Him (1 Thessalonians 4:16, 17). No advance warning preceded Enoch's departure, just as there will be no advance knowledge of the day and hour the church departs. Enoch is a picture of the righteous who will be translated in a day and an hour of which they are unaware (Matthew 24:36). This is known as the Rapture.

THE GREAT CATCHING AWAY

The Greek word in 1 Thessalonians 4:16 for "caught up" is *harpadzo*, and it means "to seize by force or to snatch out suddenly." This event is often called the Rapture, which is not in the English translation of the Bible, but is an English theological word used to describe the element of surprise and quick manner of Christ's return, when He raises the dead in Christ and catches away the believers to heaven.

Some modern teachers say that the doctrine of a "secret rapture" is not a true Biblical or historical teaching, but is a concept that was taught in the 1830's, when a woman named McDonald gave a "prophetic utterance" proclaiming two distinct appearances of Christ. Astute scholars and researchers have recently disproved the theory of a later 1830 Rapture teaching. Prior to the year 1830, Baptist Theologian Dr. John Gill, in his commentary on 1 Thessalonians 4:17, called the catching away the Rapture:

> The Apostle, having something new and extraordinary to deliver concerning the coming of Christ, the first resurrection of the saints, or the change of the living saints, and the Rapture both of the raised, and the living in the clouds to meet Christ in the air expresses itself in this manner (Dr. John Gill, *Commentary on 1 Thessalonians 4:17*).

The Eastern Orthodox Church has taught for centuries that there would be a great catching away. In fact, the writings of an Orthodox father named Ephraim the Syrian give early evidence of a pre-tribulation Rapture of the church:

> All the saints and the elect of God will be gathered together before the Tribulation, and are taken to the Lord, in order that they may not see at any time the confusion that overwhelms the world because of our sins (Ephraim the Syrian in about A.D. 373).

Scoffers and Mockers

When I hear an anti-rapture fighter mock the possibility of a pre-tribulation catching away and gathering together, I am reminded of the passage in 2 Peter that warns of scoffers in the last days saying, "Where is the promise of His coming?" (2 Peter 3:4). These skeptics are not questioning if Jesus will return, but they are questioning the *promise* of His coming.

The promise is, "I will come again and receive you to Myself, that where I am, there you may be also" (John 14:3). Never in modern history has one teaching, that of the Rapture, been so fought and hated among so-called Christians. Some go as far as to call those who believe in the Rapture heretics and teachers of doctrines of devils.

An Escape Doctrine

Scoffers mock believers, saying, "Rapture teaching is nothing more than escapism." In a literal sense, the great catching away is an escape—from the wrath of God! An examination of Scripture reveals numerous times when the righteous were permitted to escape the judgment of God. These escapes came in various forms as God separated the righteous from the unrighteous.

- Noah escaped the great flood by preparing the ark (Hebrews 11:7).
- Lot escaped the fiery judgment God sent on Sodom (Genesis 19:22).
- The Hebrew nation escaped the death angel at Passover (Exodus 12:23).
- Rahab was delivered from death in ancient Jericho (Hebrews 11:31).
- A remnant escaped Jerusalem's destruction in A.D. 70 (Luke 21:21).
- In the Tribulation, Jordan will escape the Antichrist (Daniel 11:41).
- A Jewish remnant will be sealed and protected from the Antichrist (Revelation 7:3).
- Noah, Daniel and Job could, and did, escape judgments (Ezekiel 14:13, 14).

There is a Biblical principle that the righteous believers are to be separated from the unrighteous before the judgment. An example is in Ezekiel chapter nine, when the Lord instructed an angel to mark the righteous with a special mark on their foreheads. The unrighteous were to perish in the coming judgment, but those with the special mark were to be spared from the calamity.

> "Utterly slay old and young men, maidens and little children and women; but do not come near anyone on whom is the mark; and begin at My sanctuary." So they began with the elders who were before the temple (Ezekiel 9:6).

The Rapture of the church, a teaching revealed by the Apostle Paul in the New Testament, can be seen in types, shadows and imagery throughout the Old Testament.

2. THE DEATH OF MOSES

Moses penned the first five books in the Old Testament, called the Torah. In these books, God hid the mystery of redemption in picture form through Israel's Seven Feasts (Leviticus 23). Throughout the Torah God hid future events in literal happenings that transpired.

For example, the first Passover is documented in Exodus 12. The Hebrews took a spotless male lamb and applied its blood to the doorpost in three locations (Exodus 12:7). We saw the prophetic fulfillment when Jesus, the Lamb of God, was crucified in Jerusalem near the time of the Passover. Jesus died on a cross with a cross on both sides of Him (John 19:17-19).

When Israel sinned, fiery serpents invaded the camp, biting and killing the rebels among them. Moses crafted a brass serpent on a pole. As the stricken people looked toward the brazen serpent, they were rescued from death (Numbers 21:8-9). Jesus compared his death to this historic event:

> And as Moses lifted up the serpent in the wilderness, even so must the Son of man be lifted up (John 3:14).

Conferring with Moses on Mount Sinai, God painted an astonishing picture of the future coming of Christ.

Exodus 19	*The Rapture*
God appeared on the third day	He will raise us up on the third day (Hosea 6:1-3).
God came down in the clouds	He comes in clouds (Acts 1:9, 10).
God's voice as a trumpet	The trump of God will sound (1 Thessalonians 4:16)
God's voice answered Moses	Voice of the archangel (v. 16)

God came down in fire	Christ returns with flaming fire (2 Thessalonians 1:7-10).
God descended from heaven	Christ will descend from heaven (1 Thessalonians 4:17).
God called Moses up	The saints will go up (v. 17).

Moses died before entering the Promised Land. Many Christians have died and never experienced the visible return of Christ to carry them across the Jordan River into their eternal Promised Land. After Moses died, God buried him. The Bible says, "No one knows his grave to this day" (Deuteronomy 34:6). Yet, over 1,500 years later, Moses appeared on the Mountain of Transfiguration along with Elijah (Matthew 17:1-4).

This experience, called the Transfiguration, was a preview of the resurrection of the dead. In fact, the Apostle Peter, who was sleeping prior to the event, suddenly woke up and must have imagined the resurrection of the dead had occurred. After all, there stood Moses, who had died 1,500 years before, glowing in the radiance of Christ's glory! Peter immediately desired to construct three tabernacles on the mountain (Matthew 17:4). Eventually, the vision subsided and Christ stood alone with His three inner-circle disciples.

The death of Moses before he entered the Promised Land represents those who die in Christ before the Rapture. Moses' dead body was never found, portraying the day when the dead in Christ will be raised from the grave. After 1,500 years, Moses appeared with Christ, surrounded by the glory; the dead saints will be raised by the glory of Christ and we will meet them in the air (1 Thessalonians 4:16, 17).

3. The Translation of Elijah

Elijah was one of Israel's most renowned prophets. This man of God was also translated alive into heaven in a chariot of fire, across from Jericho at the base of Mount Nebo, not far from the valley where Moses was buried (2 Kings 2: 1-12). Elijah was also the headmaster of three large schools of the prophet, prior to his ascension (2 Kings 1 and 2).

Elijah's ascension represents the Jewish remnant mentioned in the Book of Revelation. They will be caught up to the throne of God in the middle of the seven-year Tribulation (Revelation 14:1). In Revelation 7, these 144,000 Jewish men will be "sealed with the seal of God," and protected from the Antichrist (Revelation 7:3-8). Later, in chapter 14, we see these men standing before the throne of God (Revelation 14:1).

In chapter 7, these 144,000 are on earth being supernaturally sealed for protection and, in chapter 14, they are singing the song of Moses before God's throne! Obviously, at some point they were snatched out of the Tribulation and brought before God's throne. The prophet Elijah is linked to this special Jewish remnant of men. Elijah will reappear again before the great day of the Lord (Malachi 4:5).

This event is alluded to in Revelation 11, as two prophets materialize in Israel, preaching to these 144,000 men. One will be Elijah, and I believe the other will be the prophet Enoch, the only two men who escaped death in their lifetimes. After 42 months of ministry, both will be slain by the Antichrist in Jerusalem (Revelation 11:7).

These three men, Enoch, Moses and Elijah, give us a prophetic preview of events that will transpire in the future.

Enoch is a picture of the living saints who will be caught up, Moses is a picture of the dead saints whose resurrected bodies will be missing, and Elijah is a picture of the Jewish remnant that will be caught up in the middle of the Tribulation. Thus God's inspired word gives us a preview of coming events. As Solomon wrote:

> That which has been is what will be, that which is done is what will be done, and there is nothing new under the sun (Ecclesiastes 1:9).

Almighty God has performed the act of translating individuals into heaven on three occasions. Enoch was translated to heaven in Genesis 5; Elijah was translated to heaven in 2 Kings 2; and Jesus was translated to heaven in Acts 1:9. Enoch, Elijah and Jesus were all bodily carried into heaven, where they remain to this day.

Numerous individuals in Scripture were physically caught up or were given a spiritual vision of heaven. For example, Paul was caught up into the third heaven in 2 Corinthians 12:1-4, Ezekiel was caught up by the Spirit and transported in Ezekiel 10, and Phillip the evangelist was caught up from one location to another in Acts 8:39. Make no mistake, God's Word is a reliable guide.

The Bible indicates that every word is settled and established in the mouths of two or three witnesses (Deuteronomy 19:15). The inspired Word of God gives us three examples of men transported from planet earth to heaven. Both Enoch and Elijah made the journey, and are identified in the symbolism of two olive trees standing before God's throne in Zechariah 4:1-11.

Both of these ancient prophets will return to earth during the Tribulation and serve for a season as God's two witnesses in Jerusalem (Revelation 11). Jesus ascended in a cloud and was later seen in a vision by Stephen "standing on the right side of God" (Acts 7:56).

Approximately 60 years after Stephen's experience, the Apostle John again saw Christ in a heavenly vision, clothed with a white garment and standing before the seven branched menorah, representing the seven churches in Asia (Revelation 1:12-20).

This method of supernatural translation has been tested and proven three times over a period of 5,000 years. We should be encouraged that the catching away and the gathering together will be a literal event and will transpire in a day and hour when we are unaware (Matthew 24:36).

The secrets to future events were hidden in the righteous genealogies of the first 10 men in the pre-flood account in the Bible. The pattern continued with Enoch's son, Methuselah, who was the eighth man from Adam. His life and death reveal another prophesied event that will transpire prior to the return of the Lord.

CHAPTER 4

THE METHUSELAH FACTOR

The sign of water and a new flood

So all the days of Methuselah were nine hundred and sixty-nine years, and he died (Genesis 5:27).

For the earth will be filled with the knowledge of the glory of the Lord, as the waters cover the sea (Habakkuk 2:14).

For I will pour water on him who is thirsty, and floods on the dry ground. I will pour My Spirit on your descendants, and My blessing on your offspring (Isaiah 44:3).

Enoch was one of the first prophets in history. He is definitely the first man in human history to receive a divine revelation pointing to the Lord's return to earth with 10,000 of His saints (Jude 14, 15).

When this early prophet named his son Methuselah, Enoch gave the pre-flood society a child who would become a walking prophecy of future events. As previously stated, the name Methuselah signified that his death would thrust the world into judgment. Methuselah died the same year the flood erupted. Noah was 600 years old when the flood came (Genesis 7:11), and Methuselah was 969, the oldest human on record.

Seven days after Methuselah's death, the world was inundated with a universal flood—its murky waters topping the highest mountain peak by 15 cubits, or over 31 feet (Genesis 7:20). This kept anyone from surviving the deluge. Methuselah was a walking sign to the pre-flood generation that the earth would one day convulse under giant waves of water.

Prophetically, another form of water will again cover the earth in the days before the Messiah's appearance. This water is symbolically alluded to as the final outpouring of the Holy Spirit that will be poured out upon all flesh (Joel 2:28). This final deluge of God's power unleashed on humanity will begin as the birth pains leading to the Messiah's return.

THE BEGINNING OF SORROWS

Christ's disciples requested that He give them signs (events) that would occur on earth prior to His second coming. In Matthew 24, Christ listed a series of future events:

> And Jesus answered and said to them: "Take heed that no one deceives you. For many will come in My name, saying, 'I am the Christ,' and will deceive many. And you will hear of wars and rumors of wars. See that you are not troubled; for all these things must come to pass, but the end is not yet. For nation will rise against nation, and kingdom against kingdom. And there will be famines, pestilences, and earthquakes in various places. All these are the beginning of sorrows" (Mathew 24:4-8).

The first sign would be religious deception, followed by wars and rumors of wars. Wars are not a sign the end is near, but are an indication of the trouble that rabbis call the "birth pains of the Messiah."

Nation will then rise against nation and kingdom against kingdom. The Greek reads, *ethnos eppa ethnos and basileia eppa basileia.* Transliterated, ethnic race will attack ethnic race and religions will fight against other religions. Certainly, evidence of this prophecy being fulfilled is all around us.

Jesus then said, "All of these (signs) are the beginning of sorrows." The word *sorrows* is an old English word for the birth pains a woman experiences prior to the birth of her child. The Greek word here is *odin,* and is translated as "travail" in Galatians 4:19 and 1 Thessalonians 5:3. The signs mentioned above are the beginning of the birth pains. Understanding the natural birth pains helps us to comprehend the prophetic passages alluding to the spiritual birth pains.

Some skeptics note that throughout history there has always been spiritual deception, wars and rumors of wars, famines and pestilence. Why do we believe we are in the last days if these signs have always been present?

The key is not that these signs have just begun, but as with the labor pains of a woman, the closer the contractions get the sooner the baby will arrive! The frequency and intensity of these events, or the increase of the wars, famines, earthquakes, and pestilences indicate the season of the birth pains is upon us.

For example, in 1948, the year Israel again became a nation, only one large earthquake occurred. In the year 2003 alone, thousands of earthquakes were reported on the planet. The intensity and increased number of the quakes signifies that creation is "groaning and travailing" (Romans 8:22).

As the signs continue to increase in frequency and intensity, the shorter the time between the birth pains. In the natural, they begin every 10 minutes, and finally the pains seize a woman every two to three minutes. She knows the more frequently she feels the pain, the nearer the time for childbirth. The final indication that the child will soon be born is when the water breaks.

WHEN THE WATER BREAKS

When my wife, Pam, was pregnant with our son, he was born seven hours after her water broke. Our daughter was born about three hours after my wife's water broke. The breaking of water was the indication that the infant was soon to be born. Let us use this physical act of childbirth as an example to compare the death of

Methuselah to the approaching flood of Noah. As years passed and Methuselah became a very old man, this should have been a warning sign to the world that a huge volume of water was coming. Yet, none paid attention to the sign.

After the death of Methuselah, Noah was given seven days before the fountains of the deep were broken and the rain poured from heaven. Just as Methuselah was a sign of the coming rain, the Holy Spirit's rain released upon the earth is a sure sign of the soon coming of Christ. This may be why the final move of the Holy Spirit on earth is alluded to in terms of an outpouring of water and of rain. The following prophecies indicate this:

> For I will pour water upon him that is thirsty, and floods upon the dry ground: I will pour my spirit upon your seed, and my blessing upon your offspring (Isaiah 44:3).

> And it shall come to pass in the last days, says God, that I will pour out of My Spirit on all flesh; Your sons and your daughters shall prophesy. Your young men shall see visions, your old men shall dream dreams. And on My menservants and on my maidservants I will pour out My Spirit in those days; and they shall prophesy (Acts 2:17, 18).

> Therefore be patient, brethren, until the coming of the Lord. See how the farmer waits for the precious fruit of the earth, waiting patiently for it until it receives the early and latter rain. You also be patient. Establish your hearts, for the coming of the Lord is at hand (James 5:7, 8).

THE EARLY AND LATTER RAIN

In ancient Israel, Jews were familiar with the terms "early and latter rain." The early rain came in order to prepare the ground for the seed and the latter rain came at harvest time (Deuteronomy 11:14). The first major outpouring of the Holy Spirit came on the Feast of Pentecost in Acts 2:1-4 to bring spiritual power to the disciples and to birth the church. This was the season when the seed of the new Covenant was being planted throughout the world. As the endtime gospel is spread across the world, another outpouring of the latter rain of the Holy Spirit can be expected, to help ripen the hearts of humanity and bring in the final harvest of the lost into the kingdom of God.

The early rains begin during the fall months of late October and early November, never suddenly but by various degrees. Usually, the rains continue for two or three days at a time, especially at night. This gives the farmer time to plow his field and plant the wheat and barley. Once the seed is planted, under normal circumstances the rains become steady during the late winter months.

The early rain prepares the dry ground to receive the seed and the latter rain, which peaks around March or April, helps to mature and ripen the barley and the wheat for the harvest. Historically, the early rain occurred at the birth of the church and the latter rain will occur before the catching away of the church. Both Holy Spirit outpourings are for the maturing of the spiritual harvest of souls, bringing the "wheat" into the church.

God predicted He would *pour out His spirit upon all flesh,* in the last days (Acts 2:17-18). The first outpouring of the Spirit came on mature men and women who had gathered in an upper room to seek God (Acts 1:13; Luke 24:49). The latter rain outpouring will come on our sons and our daughters (Acts 2:17, 18).

The early rain fell on the dry, barren hearts of the Hebrew nation as the seed of God's word was planted in Jerusalem, Judea, Samaria, and the uttermost parts of the earth (Acts 1:8). The latter rain will help ripen the hearts of people around the world and prepare the final great harvest of souls for the kingdom of God (James 5:7).

NO RAIN THEOLOGY

Some liberal theologians are convinced there will be no final outpouring of the Holy Spirit on the earth before Christ's return. They accept the "no rain theology" that says all miracles, supernatural gifts and divine manifestations of the Holy Spirit were relegated to the first century church.

Others proclaim that with the completion of the New Testament, there was no longer a necessity for any spiritual manifestation through the Holy Spirit. Some point out that historically, miracles began to decline by the fourth century, so that becomes their proof that miracles have ceased.

I contend that there is no such thing as a season of miracles, but God performs the miracles. If miracles ceased, then God no longer answers prayer; any form of answered prayer is a miracle to those who receive the answer. Secondly, no scripture indicates that miracles will cease during the church age. In fact, we are told that the "gifts" of the Spirit (Greek *chrisma*) will continue until the coming of the Lord.

> So that ye come behind in no gift; waiting for the coming of our Lord Jesus Christ (1 Corinthians 1:7).

The gifts of the Holy Spirit are for the edification, exhortation and comfort of the church. Since the church is still alive and well on earth, there is a consistent need for spiritual edification, exhortation and comfort. When we are made perfect at the return of Christ and receive our glorified bodies, then and only then will there be no need for the supernatural gifts. At that time, they will cease (1 Corinthians 13:10).

I believe this is why God said that in the last days He would pour His Spirit (the latter rain) on the sons and the daughters. Often, older Christians become set in their spiritual ways and are not open-minded to any teaching that may appear contrary to their own pre-conceived denominational interpretations.

Occasionally, I have watched seasoned adults walk out of a service because a minister was preaching something they didn't agree with. Instead of searching the Scriptures as the men of Berea did in the New Testament, to obtain a clearer understanding of the truth (Acts17:10, 11), some build a wall of denominationalism above the scriptures and refuse to listen to anything that would challenge their opinions or change their understanding.

WHY THE SONS AND DAUGHTERS?

This is why sons and daughters will accept the final outpouring of the Spirit. The younger generation is open to hear truth and Biblical teaching that has been hidden, either willfully or ignorantly, from them. During many years of ministry, I have personally met thousands of young born-again, Spirit-filled firebrands for the Kingdom of God; yet their own parents don't attend church or they occasionally attend a formal, politically-correct church on Sunday mornings and have no interest in their children's spiritual growth. Today's youth are not easily intimidated or embarrassed. They freely and openly discuss almost any subject without blushing and desire to attend a church that has spiritual life and not just attend church because it is a family custom.

It will be the youth of this final generation who will initiate and participate in the final outpouring of the Holy Spirit on earth. In most nations outside of America and Canada, the majority of Christians filling the churches are under 30 years of age. In Africa, South America, Indonesia and many third world countries, the average age of churchgoers is no longer older people, but youth.

THREE SIGNS IN THIS GENERATION

I believe this is the generation of the outpouring of the Holy Spirit for three reasons: The sign of the birth pain (Matthew 24:8), the sign of the end-time harvest (Matthew 13:39), and the sign of the global outpouring of the Holy Spirit (Acts 2:17, 18).

The first indicator is the sign of the birth pains. When the signs of Mathew 24 climax, it is the beginning of the birth pains. Prior to the return of Christ, the spiritual water must break. In the natural, when a woman's travail reaches a peak, her water will break. This is the final sign that a child will soon be born. The breaking of the water before Christ's return is a picture of the final outpouring of the latter rain of the Spirit! Remember, the Holy Spirit is compared to water, rain and an out-pouring of rain. Paul spoke about being in travail until Christ is formed in us (Galatians 4:19).

Secondly, the latter rain outpouring of the Spirit upon our sons and daughters is a visible sign that the final harvest of souls is near. It is the latter rain that helps the fruit of the field to mature and grow. It comes before the main harvest. Without this rain, the ground would be dry, the seed would perish and there would be no harvest. The Holy Spirit comes to moisten the seed of the Word, and help it to take root into the human spirit. He brings anointing and power to the preached Word, enabling us to hear and feel the presence of God.

According to Christ, the harvest is the "end of the age" (Matthew 13:39). In this harvest parable, the reapers represent ministers, going forth preaching the gospel to all nations and bringing souls into the Kingdom of God. Just as the natural latter rains prepare the barley and wheat for the harvest, so the Holy Spirit is using believers in the church to reach a massive global harvest of souls. This harvest is to be swept into the kingdom of God at the end of this age!

The third sign is the global outpouring of the Holy Spirit. Often Christians in America judge what God is doing by the visible spiritual activity in America. Those doing this are looking through a narrow set of Western glasses and do not understand the magnitude of God's Kingdom on earth.

I once had lunch with a former General Overseer in a major Pentecostal denomination. He said to me, "I always saw the church through denominational glasses. I never knew how large and powerful the Body of Christ was, until I got out from under the denomination and began traveling throughout the world, listening to and sitting under other ministries." Outside North America, there are nations where literally hundreds of thousands of believers are members of one church!

In this last day outpouring of the rain of the Spirit, it is wonderful to see how the Spirit of God has demonstrated His power in nations that have been sealed off from Western missionary influences. Under 70 years of cruel Communist dictatorship, the underground Pentecostal churches in Russia, Bulgaria, and Romania continued to flourish and grow.

The same is true with China and Vietnam. China has a population of over a billion people, and some sources estimate there may be as many as 100 million secret Christians in this Communist stronghold. Even in Vietnam, underground Christians meet in secret locations in the mountains to pray and worship. The same is true in strong Islamic countries. Dictators and religious oppressors might keep the Bible out of their countries and forbid Christian worship and religious gatherings, but they cannot restrain the work of the Holy Spirit as He secretly invades these strongholds of religious oppression.

Now or Later

I have heard prophetic teachers relegate these promises of the Holy Spirit being poured out to a past event, a fulfillment in the first century, or either a future fulfillment after Satan is bound during the one thousand year rule of Christ. Those teaching this doctrine are often good men, but they have been educated in seminaries that teach miracles and spiritual gifts have ceased. But anyone who examines the promises of the outpouring of the Spirit must see that there will be an outpouring prior to the return of Jesus Christ.

This outpouring will occur now, rather than later. Just as the death of Methuselah was a sign that the water was coming, the signs of the last days indicate that there is another form of water, a flood of the Holy Spirit's power that will be released before the return of Christ. The water of the Spirit is needed to nourish the dry soil of men's hearts so they can receive the seed of God's Word. The rain is coming again!

CHAPTER 5

UNUSUAL CLUES WITH NOAH AND LOT

Important keys to the coming of Christ

But as the days of Noah were, so also will the coming of the Son of Man be. For as in the days before the flood, they were eating and drinking, marrying and giving in marriage, until the day that Noah entered the ark, and did not know until the flood came and took them all away, so also will the coming of the Son of Man be. Then two men will be in the field: one will be taken and the other left. Two women will be grinding at the mill; one will be taken and the other left. Watch therefore, for you do not know what hour our Lord is coming. But know this, that if the master of the house had known what hour the thief would come, he would have watched and not allowed his house to be broken into. Therefore you also be ready, for the Son of Man is coming at an hour you do not expect (Matthew 24:37-44).

esus compared the season of His return to earth to the days of Lot and Noah. After years of research, I have discovered that there are numerous clues hidden within the stories of Noah and Lot, which reveal a deeper insight into the mystery of Christ's return to earth. Noah and Lot were righteous men (Genesis 6:9, 2 Peter 2:7, 8). Both men escaped the judgment God sent upon their generation and both were concerned about their families that they, too, would escape the wrath to come (Hebrews 11:7, Genesis 19:14).

Thus far we have observed how the seventh generation man, Enoch, was caught up alive into heaven. The number seven indicates completion or perfection and has been called "God's perfect number." The seventh man from Adam could allude to the 7,000 years of human government and the seventh millennium, which will introduce the future catching away of the church.

- The eighth man from Adam was Methuselah. The Biblical number *eight* alludes to new beginnings.

- The death of the eighth man from Adam introduced a new world to Noah and his sons.

- There were eight family members in Noah's ark who, after the flood, repopulated a new world (1 Peter 3:20).

- Later, God instructed Abraham that a Jewish male child was to be circumcised on the eighth day after his birth, as a sign of entering into covenant with the Almighty (Genesis 17:12).

- Jesus appeared after eight days to His disciples and Thomas, in order to reveal His new, resurrected body (John 20:26).

If the seventh millennium initiates the rule of Christ, then the eighth millennium could possibly introduce the *new* heaven and the *new* earth with the holy city New Jerusalem coming down from God out of heaven (Revelation 21:1-3).

Noah was the 10th generation from Adam. The name Noah in Hebrew is *Noach*, and means "rest." The Biblical number *10* is associated with government, judgment and divine order. There were 10 plagues that hit the Egyptians (Exodus 3-12), and there were Ten Commandments given to Israel (Exodus 34:28). Through Noah, the 10th man from Adam, God brought divine judgment to the world and set a new world into a divine order, using one righteous man and his family!

Patterns in the Ten Generations

A unique pattern begins to develop in the Bible when we begin counting every 10th generation from Adam. According to Moses in Genesis 5, here are the first 10 men from Adam through the righteous lineage of Seth, in the order in which they were born:

Name	Reference
Adam	v. 5
Seth	v. 8
Enos	v. 11
Cainan	v. 14
Mahalaleel	v. 15
Jared	v. 20
Enoch	v. 24
Methuselah	v. 27
Lamech	v. 31
Noah	v. 32

The 10th generation from Adam concluded with a global flood that destroyed mankind, with the exception of Noah and his family. After the flood, the first righteous generation to repopulate the earth was through the lineage of Shem, Noah's oldest son (Genesis 6:10). When we begin with Shem and move forward 10 generations, we see another divinely orchestrated event beginning to unfold. This is the list of the 10 generations beginning with Shem:

Name	Reference
Shem	Genesis 11:11
Arphaxad	v. 13
Salah	v. 15
Eber	v. 17
Peleg	v. 19
Reu	v. 21
Serug	v. 23
Nahor	v. 24
Terah	v. 25
Abraham	v. 26

After the universal deluge, the 10th generation through Seth's lineage was Abraham. Abraham would form a new nation and become the father of the covenant. From Abraham's seed would come the mighty nation of Israel (Genesis 12:7; 15:18; 17:8). Abraham was father to Isaac, who fathered a son called Jacob, who became the father of twelve sons identified as the twelve tribes of Israel.

If we begin with Abraham's son, Isaac, and we move forward 10 more generations, another pattern begins to emerge. Again we turn to the Biblical genealogies listing the 10 generations beginning with Isaac. This time we

will glean our information from the genealogies recorded
in the New Testament, in Matthew's gospel. Beginning
with Isaac and moving forward 10 men, we see these
names listed:

Isaac	Matthew 1:2
Jacob	v. 2
Judah	v. 2
Phares	v. 3
Esrom	v. 3
Aram	v. 3
Aminadab	v. 4
Naasom	v. 4
Salmon	v. 4
Boaz	v. 5

The 10th generation from Isaac was Boaz. The story of
Boaz is found in the Old Testament Book of Ruth. This
beautiful love story, involving Boaz and Ruth, is a prophetic picture of how Christ, our heavenly Boaz, would
one day redeem a Gentile bride that would become His
church! Comparing Boaz and Ruth to Christ and the
church, we see several interesting parallels:

- ◆ Boaz was from Bethlehem, and Christ was born
  in Bethlehem.
- ◆ Boaz was from the tribe of Judah, and Christ
  was from Judah.
- ◆ Boaz worked in the fields, and Christ spoke of
  the harvest.
- ◆ Boaz chose a wife who was a Gentile, and Christ
  chose a Gentile bride.
- ◆ Boaz was a kinsman-redeemer, and Christ was
  our Kinsman-Redeemer.
- ◆ Boaz married Ruth, and we are espoused (married) to Christ.

♦ From Boaz and Ruth came King David, from Christ comes a royal priesthood

THE MISSING *VAV* IS RESTORED

Another interesting aspect to the story of Ruth and Boaz is found when we examine the Hebrew word for generations, located in Ruth 4:18. The first time the word *generations* is used in the Bible is when God completed the creation process and saw that it was good. The Scripture states:

> These are the generations of the heavens and of the earth when they were created, in the day that the Lord God made the earth and the heavens (Genesis 2:4, KJV).

The Hebrew word for generations is *toledah*. The Hebrew letter *vav* is found in the Hebrew spelling of this word. This sixth letter of the Hebrew alphabet is actually found twice in the Hebrew spelling of the word *generations* in Genesis 2:4. After Adam's sin and his expulsion from the Garden of Eden, the word *generations* is used again in Genesis 5:1:

> This is the book of the generations of Adam. In the day that God created man, in the likeness of God made he him (Genesis 5:1, KJV).

Here, the second *vav* is missing in the spelling of the Hebrew Scriptures. Since the symbol of the letter *vav* is a hook, the letter symbolizes a connector. God is telling the reader (in Hebrew) that Adam's fall has crippled his connection with God. Throughout the five books of Moses (the Torah), the word *generations* is spelled with the second *vav* missing (Genesis 6:9, 9:12, 10:1, 10:32, 11:10, 11:27, 17:7, 17:12, 25:12). This is true in 61 other places where the word *generations* is written.

In the story of Boaz and Ruth, after they were married and began having children, the missing *vav* reappears in the Hebrew text in Ruth 4:18:

> Now these are the generations of Pharez: Pharez begat Hezron (Ruth 4:18, KJV).

The word *generations* in this passage is spelled in the same manner as in Genesis 2:4, when God completed His creative process (see the Hebrew chart in the center of the book). Some have questioned why the perfect spelling reappears here and not in some earlier passage. It is because through Ruth and Boaz a descendant would be born named David, and through David's seed the throne of Jerusalem was promised. In fact, the future Messiah was called the son of David (Matthew 1:1).

David was the 33rd generation from Adam, according to Biblical chronology. Solomon, David's son, was the 34th generation from Adam. Solomon built the Temple in Jerusalem, and they experienced 40 years of peace and prosperity under his reign. It is interesting to note that most scholars believe Christ was 33, or slightly older, when He was crucified in Jerusalem for the sins of mankind. Through His death, He became our high priest in the heavenly Temple, giving us access to God's Presence. As the Messiah, son of David, Christ will return in the future and rule from a new Temple in Jerusalem (Ezekiel 44-47).

THE TEN GENERATIONS

Remember that the Biblical number 10 can allude to government, judgment or divine order.

- The 10th generation from Adam was Noah, who saw the world judged and a new governmental order initiated by the Almighty.

- The 10th generation from Seth was Abraham, the principle patriarch whose covenant with God would bring about the birth of the nation of Israel, through his son, Isaac and his son, Jacob.
- The 10th generation from Isaac was Boaz who became a kinsman-redeemer and married a Gentile woman. Their lineage produced David, the king to whom God promised an everlasting kingdom.
- Prophetically, the 10th person in the early genealogies either encountered God's judgment or helped to initiate a major prophetic assignment, releasing God's divine plan on earth.
- Genesis 8:5 says the flood waters decreased in the 10th month.
- The number 10 can also be found when researching the Biblical narrative related to Lot and the destruction of Sodom and Gomorrah.

According to Christ, many clues related to His return are found in the stories of Noah and Lot (Luke 17:26-29).

LOOKING FOR TEN RIGHTEOUS ONES

God informed Abraham He would destroy the twin cities of Sodom and Gomorrah. Before their judgment, the Lord sent angels to Abraham informing him of the upcoming calamity. Abraham became concerned about his nephew Lot who, along with his family, was dwelling in the city of Sodom.

Abraham began negotiating with the Lord, asking Him to spare the city if 50 righteous were found among the population (Genesis 18:24). The Lord agreed (v. 26).

Abraham began lowering the number down from 50 to 40, to 30, to 20, and finally concluded with 10.

> Then he said, "Let not the Lord be angry, and I will speak but once more: suppose ten should be found there?" And He said, "I will not destroy it for the sake of ten" (v. 32).

Why did Abraham end his negotiating by stopping with only 10 righteous people? Months before this negotiation, Lot and Abraham had separated from one another. The land could not contain the growth of their flocks. After this division, it appears Lot moved 10 members of his family into the wicked city.

The Bible records four people coming out, instead of the 10 Abraham had suggested. We know that Lot, his wife, and two daughters came out of the city prior to Sodom's destruction. However, according to Genesis 19:14, Lot was instructed to warn several daughters and sons-in-laws living within the city, of the impending judgment from God:

> So Lot went out and spoke to his sons-in-law, who had married his daughters, and said, "Get up, get out of this place; for the Lord will destroy this city!" But to his sons-in-law he seemed to be joking.

Lot's daughters and sons-in-law were soon consumed in the fiery destruction of the cities. Lot escaped with two of his daughters. His wife perished on the way out, as she looked back to watch the burning cities (Genesis 19:26).

It appears that several daughters of Lot, perhaps three, had married men in Sodom. The ungodly influence of the wicked men in this perverted city had somehow corrupted the minds of some of Lot's children. The warning of destruction was perceived as a practical joke. Just as in Noah's time, because there was no visible warning that destruction would soon follow, the world's population ignored the message. Why would they heed the ranting of two men—one building a floating zoo and one claiming a city would soon be wiped out?

THE FAMILY—SOME LOST, SOME SAVED

The return of Christ is compared to the days of Lot and Noah (Luke 17:26-29). Both men were concerned about their immediate family and both informed their blood line about the coming disasters.

Noah had 100 years to prepare his family, but Lot had only a day. Noah successfully secured his entire family (his wife, three sons, and their wives) into the ark and they were preserved during the violent, universal flood (2 Peter 2:5). Lot, on the other hand, appears to have had at least 10 family members, and over half were destroyed in the fires of destruction in Sodom.

How was Noah able to convince his entire household to heed the warnings, and Lot was unable to persuade his daughters and sons-in-law? The answer may be found when examining Lot's reaction to the men of Sodom.

In Lot's day, as today, there was a huge homosexual population living in the heart of the city. When the two angels, who appeared in the form of men, entered Lot's house, a violent mob of gay men surrounded the front of Lot's door and demanded he release the strangers to them for their sexual pleasure:

> Now before they lay down, the men of the city, the men of Sodom, both old and young, all the people from every quarter, surrounded the house. And they called to Lot and said to him, "Where are the men who came to you tonight? Bring them out to us that we may know them carnally" (Genesis 19:4, 5).

Lot immediately responded in a manner that is unthinkable. He called these men "brethren" (v. 7), and then offered them his two virgin daughters to "do with them what they please" (v. 8). This action indicates Lot was willing to compromise with the wicked men in the city, instead of taking a righteous stand and rebuking them for their wickedness.

This spirit of compromise may be why he had lost influence over his daughters and sons-in-law when he ran to their home saying, "We must get out because God is going to destroy this place!" (vv. 13, 14). In Noah's day, the same type of perversion and immorality surrounded him and his family. The Bible says that violence had filled the earth and that men's imagination was evil continually (Genesis 6:5-11). However, the filth of Noah's generation never filtered into the lives of his sons.

By Noah keeping his family active in preparing the ark, they had little time for carnal pleasures. While the men in Noah's generation were getting drunk, chasing women, and telling their unclean stories, Noah and his three sons were chopping down trees, hewing logs, mixing tar and preparing an enormous floating houseboat.

If we can keep our children and families involved in the work of God's kingdom, they will have less time to fellowship with workers of darkness and become familiar with the "men of Sodom!" The prophet Ezekiel states that idleness was one of the sins of Sodom:

> Look, this was the iniquity of your sister Sodom: She and her daughter had pride, fullness of food, and abundance of idleness; neither did she strengthen the hand of the poor and needy (Ezekiel 16:49).

The old timers used to say, "Idleness is the devil's workshop." When people have excessive time, they can become busybodies and gossips; they can waste time engaging with the wrong people.

The Importance of the Door

The second significant observation involves the door. Noah's ark had a large door, just as Lot's home in Sodom had a front door. The purpose of any door is to enhance security for those behind the door, and prevent intruders from entering. A closed door is a barrier to what is on the outside. In Noah's day, that wicked generation of filthy thinkers did not enter the ark. However, in Lot's generation, he actually opened his door to converse with the mob of sexual perverts.

Both Noah and Lot had family members behind their doors. The difference was that Noah controlled what came into his ark by regulating the door. Lot compromised his sacred boundaries because he felt threatened by the men of Sodom, thus opening the door to converse and compromise with the men of the city.

> And Lot went out at the door unto them, and shut the door after him. And they pressed sore upon the man, even Lot, and came near to break the door. But the men put forth their hand, and pulled Lot into the house to them, and shut the door (Genesis 19:6, 9, 10, KJV)

Lot's mistake was not supervising access to the door of his house. When the men began knocking, Lot opened the door to evil men who felt the freedom to have access to those in Lot's house. Because of fear, and to protect the two strangers in his house, Lot offered an unimaginable compromise. He proposed the men of Sodom take his two virgin daughters and rape them throughout the night, and not have homosexual relations with the men.

> See now, I have two daughters who have not known a man;
> please, let me bring them out to you, and you may do to them
> as you wish; only do nothing to these men, since this is the
> reason they have come under the shadow of my roof (v. 8).

This moment of compromise paints a sad picture of a righteous man (2 Peter 2:8). His compromise impacted the thinking of his two daughters to the point that after the demise of Sodom and the death of their mother, both daughters conspired to get their father drunk and conceived sons through him. One named her son *Moab,* and the other was named *Benammi* (Genesis 19:37, 38).

Any father willing to turn his daughters over to a gang of sex-thirsty men might as well expect the daughters to be willing to compromise their own convictions. It appears that Noah was a strong leader with great influence over his family. Lot, however, was a compromiser and it cost him his integrity and much of his family.

- ♦ Lot's sons-in-law mocked him.
- ♦ Lot offered his daughters to be raped by a gang of homosexual men.
- ♦ Lot had no influence over his wife, since she looked back and was destroyed.
- ♦ Lot's daughters had no respect for their father, as he fathered two sons through them.

In the examples of Noah and Lot, the door was an opening into a place of security. Not only is the door literal, but it can also represent the entrance into the human mind and spirit. We have three gates into our inner man— the eyes, ears and mouth. This represents what we see, hear and speak. We must continually guard these three doors that lead into our souls and spirits.

The spiritual importance of the door is seen in two other Old Testament examples.

Protection in the House

The importance of the door can be found in the story of Passover, and the amazing account of God's supernatural protection of the harlot Rahab and her family in the ancient city of Jericho.

During the first Passover, God instructed every Hebrew family to place three marks of lamb's blood on the posts of their doors. They were commanded to stay in the house as the death angel swept through the land at midnight. God said, "And none of you shall go out of the door of his house until the morning" (Exodus 12:22).

The reason was so that the destroyer would not have access to kill any firstborn Hebrew son (Exodus 12:29). Total family protection was provided to every Hebrew under the condition that their families remained in the house "under the blood of the lamb!"

In the second account, Rahab was a harlot whose house was built upon the walls of Jericho, a strong Canaanite city once nestled in the Jordan Valley (Joshua 2:15). Rahab secretly hid two Hebrew spies in her house and demanded a promise from them that, because of her faith in the Hebrew God, they would protect her when the city was seized.

Rahab was instructed to place a scarlet thread in her window and that she and her family were to remain in the house when the war and fighting broke out. She was also warned, "So it shall be that whoever goes outside the doors of your house into the street, his blood shall be on his own head, and we will be guiltless" (Joshua 2:19).

In both Biblical narratives, keeping the door closed and remaining in the house guaranteed the family's total protection from the destruction on the outside. The lesson from Noah's ark is to control who and what comes into the door.

The lesson from Lot's day is that we should refuse to open the door to anything that introduces perversion or division in our homes. Christian parents are responsible for protecting the minds of their children from the perverse influences on the outside of the home.

This is why many Christian parents home-school or send their children to a Christian school. Christian parents who home-school their children, guard what their children watch on television, and protect them from dangerous "friends" are often called fanatics and are criticized as narrow-minded.

Yet, few of their children become drug dealers, prostitutes, or end up costing the taxpayers by spending a few years behind bars! These parents are controlling the doors of their home and, by the grace of God, will save their house from the day of trouble! If Lot had controlled the door, perhaps all 10 of his family members could have been spared.

THE TEN VIRGINS

The number 10 is connected to the judgment of Sodom, and is also a number used in a famous parable in the New Testament related to the return of the Lord. This story, recognized as the Parable of the Ten Virgins (Matthew 25:1-10), may give us a clue as to how many will remain faithful until Christ comes and the number that may remain behind at the gathering together of the church in heaven.

The concept of 10 virgins was not a foreign teaching to Christ's followers. His Jewish audience was fully aware of the Hebrew wedding customs and the role that 10 virgins played in an actual Jewish wedding. Once a Jewish man was engaged to a young woman, they were considered legally married. However, the marriage was not consummated until many months later, after the groom completed a dwelling place for the couple to live in.

Between the initial engagement, called the *kiddushin*, and the actual wedding celebration, called the *nisu'in*, the bride would wear a veil and surround herself with 10 young virgins who would help keep her excited about her future wedding. They would ensure that her garments were clean and that a special oil lamp was prepared in the event the groom would appear at night and receive her unto him.

Each of the 10 virgins was given a long pole with an oil lamp attached to the top. During the night, they were to remain prepared with oil in their lamps and an extra vial of oil in case the groom would secretly arrive late at night to receive his bride. In the parable, they all expected the husband of the bride to come at midnight, but for some reason he was delayed. Because the hour was late, all 10 virgins became weary of waiting and fell asleep. Suddenly, the announcement came that the bridegroom was coming! The 10 virgins quickly arose, trimmed the wicks in the lamps, but five had forgotten one important item—the extra oil (Mathew 25:7-8).

As the five wise virgins poured reserve oil into their lamps, the five who were lacking oil asked to borrow more oil from the other five, but there was not enough. The five lacking oil were told to go buy oil. As they were busy with their business, the bridegroom came and they were left behind. Once again we see a door is connected to the story:

> And while they went to buy, the bridegroom came, and those who were ready went in with him to the wedding; and the door was shut (v. 10).

In this parable, half of the group was prepared and half was not. In Noah's day, he saved his entire household; but in Lot's day, he lost over half of his family as judgment fell. Just as in the parable there were 10 virgins, we can assume Lot had 10 in the family. Some were wise and others were foolish. One of the sad commentaries about Lot's family was the loss of his wife moments before the family was drawn into the mountains and saved.

REMEMBER LOT'S WIFE

When Jesus compared the signs of His coming to the days of Lot, He interjected this statement: "Remember Lot's wife" (Luke 17:32). In the Genesis account, the angels warned Lot, his wife, and daughters not to look back. As the cities began to burn, Lot's wife looked back and "became a pillar of salt" (Genesis 19:26).

I have personally stood at the Dead Sea where this event happened. The southern part of the Dead Sea, where the cities once existed, is currently a reservoir containing salt and chemicals. In fact, I have stood at the base of a huge mountain that is several hundred feet high and it is one solid piece of salt! Geological evidence suggests that there was once a huge volcanic eruption at the southern end of the Dead Sea.

Some have speculated that as this explosion occurred, tons of water from the Dead Sea shot into the atmosphere and came crashing down. The high volume of chemical and salt content would form salt crystals in a short time, just as it does today when the current from the Dead Sea water forms salt crystals on the rocks near the edge of the Dead Sea. Thus Lot's wife was too close to the judgment (the explosion) to be spared from it. This is why Lot was commanded to get to the mountain, away from the falling fire and brimstone.

What are the lessons to be learned from Lot's wife? *I believe the first lesson is that once you receive Christ, don't look back.* Even the Apostle Paul wrote, "Forgetting those things which are behind...press towards the mark..." (Philippians 3:13). The writer of Hebrews also said, "We are not of them that draw back into perdition but them that believe in the saving of the soul" (Hebrews 10:39). My wife, Pam, has often said, "What is there to look back for?" Remember, no man who puts his hand to the plow and looks back is fit to enter the kingdom of God (Luke 9:62).

The second lesson is there will be people, as in the Parable of the Ten Virgins, who will be on the verge of preparing for the great escape from the coming tribulation, but at the last minute they will turn back and not be prepared for Christ's sudden appearance. Perhaps even on the day of Christ's return, they will look back as Lot's wife did. Christ warned about this:

> But take heed to yourselves, lest your hearts be weighed down with carousing, drunkenness, and cares of this life, and that day come on you unexpectedly. For it will come as a snare on all those who dwell on the face of the whole earth. Watch therefore, and pray always that you may be counted worthy to escape all these things that will come to pass, and to stand before the Son of Man (Luke 21:34-36).

When Jesus admonished us to remember Lot's wife, I believe He was warning us not to turn back once we set our hearts to separate ourselves from the cares of the world and the deceitfulness found in the earth's major cities. The lights, the glitz and the amusements will not save us in the time of the end.

Cosmic Signs in Noah's Day and Today

As indicated in this chapter, there are many clues related to Christ's return found in the stories of Noah and Lot. Recent research also indicates some amazing parallels corresponding to the days prior to the flood and our present age. A series of cosmic signs is part of these parallels.

Jesus said there would be signs in the "sun, moon, and stars" prior to His return (Luke 21:25). The Bible teaches that God created the lights in the heavens for signs and seasons (Genesis 1:14). Notice that He also made them for days and years. "Days and years" seems to be distinguished from "signs and seasons." Why is this?

The Hebrew root of the word used here for "signs" is *ote*. Not only does it mean "sign," but also can allude to a warning or an omen. The root of the word used for seasons is *moed*. The word *moed* means "appointed time" and is used in the Bible most frequently to describe the seven Biblical festivals: Passover, Pentecost, Tabernacles, and so forth. God's intention for the sun, moon and stars was, and is, more than just calculating days and years.

A primary purpose for the celestial bodies is to give us warnings about appointed times. The ancient Hebrew calendar was calculated using a lunar system based upon the positioning of the moon. Certain feasts fell on days in which there was a new moon. In fact, the months were determined by the position of the new moon.

WHEN THE MOON BECOMES BLOOD

For centuries, Jewish sources have noted the significance of lunar and solar eclipses. The Jewish Talmud has a lot to say on the subject of lunar eclipses. In *Sukkah 29a* it is written, "When the moon is in eclipse, it is a bad omen for Israel . . . if the face is as red as blood, (it is a sign) the sword is coming to the world."

In 1996, two lunar eclipses fell on major Jewish feast days. The first happened on Passover of that year, followed months later by another lunar eclipse that fell on the eve of the Feast of Tabernacles (September 27, 1996) and was referred to in Israeli newspapers as a "bloody moon" (Joel 2:31). In a strange and rare coincidence, a 90 percent eclipse of the moon happened in March of 1997 on Purim, and a minor eclipse happened on September 16, 1997, which fell in the middle of a time known as the "Days of Repentance."

The fact that these lunar eclipses fell on major Jewish Feast days was a sign to the Rabbis throughout the world that something very big would transpire in the near future. Four years later, America was struck with the biggest terrorist attack in her history, thrusting our nation into a massive war against global terrorists and their networks. The attack on September 11 has so far led to wars in Afghanistan and Iraq.

In Hebrew tradition, a full blood moon means a "sword is coming to the world." The Bible speaks of the "moon becoming as blood" (Revelation 6:12). The moon could never be covered with literal blood; therefore, there is a hidden meaning in this prophecy. That meaning, in line with Hebrew tradition, alludes to total lunar eclipses when the moon appears to be a blood-red color.

The Return of the Comets

Another interesting sign relates to the appearance of comets. One recent comet that drew much attention was the Hale-Bopp comet, which passed through our solar system during a very important prophetic season. From earth, the Hale-Bopp comet appeared nearly 50,000 times brighter than the famous Halley's Comet.

Hale-Bopp was discovered on July 23, 1995, in the heavenly constellation Sagittarius. The February 14, 1997 issue of *PSR Discoveries* reported that "On August 2, 1995 . . . pre-discovery images were found on photographic plates taken at the Anglo-Australian Observatory on April 27, 1993. The images showed that the comet was active." It was found that the previous passage of this comet was 4,200 years ago. Christian astronomers such as Bob Wadsworth believe this was the same comet that Jewish tradition indicates was seen when Noah was building the ark! The *Sedar Olam Rabbah,* an ancient Jewish text, states that a comet appeared in the heavens at the time of the building of the ark.

Assuming this was the same comet, was the reappearing of this unknown comet a heavenly warning that we were entering the days of Noah, and we should be preaching a warning message to this generation and preparing our families for future events?

Another interesting link between this comet and Noah is the time frame in which the comet was visible to those of us living on earth. The earliest visible evidence we have of the comet's reappearance was acquired on April 27, 1993. That date on the Hebrew calendar was the 6th of Iyar. This is interesting because this date and year on the Hebrew calendar was the 45-year anniversary of the year the British mandate over Palestine ended and the re-birth of Israel as a nation. That date was May 15, 1948!

The peak visibility for the comet was the year 1998. October 2, 1998 marked the beginning of the Hebrew year 5758. The Hebrew alphabet is often interchanged with numbers. The numbers 58 consist of two Hebrew letters, nun and chet. Together these two letters spell the Hebrew name for Noah! If we go back 4,200 years from 5758, we come to the Jewish year of 1558, or the time that Noah was making preparation for the ark.

When translating the Hebrew year 1558 into the al-phabet, the letters form the Hebrew word *kinach*. This word means to "wipe clean." It conveys the idea of start-ing over again. God told Noah, "The end of all flesh is come before me...I will destroy them with the earth" (Gen-esis 6:13). The message hidden in the Hebrew date 1558 alludes to the fact that God was going to "wipe" the earth clean and start over with Noah and his family!

MORE UNUSUAL COSMIC SINGS

If we are to discern the true cosmic signs in the heav-ens pointing to Christ's return, we must acknowledge that God created the constellations in the heavens and God has an original intended purpose and meaning for them. The heavens declare the glory of God, according to Psalms 19:1. Even the inspired Scriptures mention several of the constellations by name, such as Orion, Arcturus, and the Pleiades (Job 9:9, 38:31; Amos 5:8).

The Hale-Bopp comet was first discovered while it was traveling through the constellation Sagittarius. Sagit-tarius is the bow-wielding archer who is seen as the coming conqueror. Could the discovery of Hale-Bopp within this particular constellation allude to the coming of the Antichrist predicted in Revelation? Is it possible that this constellation alludes to the Beast referred to in Revelation 13, who is also identified as an archer in Revelation 6:2?

Sagittarius has two natures—one beast, one man—just as the future Antichrist is a human but is identified in the symbolism of a beast in Revelation 13:1. By studying the course Hale-Bopp has taken through the heavens, this Antichrist theme materializes in greater detail.

After Hale-Bopp left Sagittarius, it made its way toward the constellation Perseus. Specifically, it crossed the section of Perseus known as "the severed head of Gorgon," Medusa. In Hebrew this is known as Rosh Satan, "The head of Satan." The principal star in this part of the constellation is the variable star Al Gol. The name of this star means "the evil spirit."

By comparing the paths of Hale-Bopp and another comet called Hyakutake, you will discover that their paths intersected near Al Gol, in the "head of Satan." Hyakutake was at this point on April 11, 1996. Hale-Bopp was also at this point on April 11, 1997! Their intersecting paths form an X in the forehead of the "head of Satan."

Could this be a cosmic sign alluding to the coming mark of the beast in Revelation 13:16, which men will receive in their right hands or in their heads?

Perseus is a decan, or division, of the constellation Aries. In Hebrew, Aries is called *Taleh* and means "lamb." This lamb is pictured with two horns. It seems that not only could this "lamb" allude to the lamb of God, but also to the "lamb with two horns" mentioned in the Apocalypse (Revelation 13:11). Directly below Aries is the constellation Cetus, the sea monster.

In his classic book, *Witness of the Stars*, E.W. Bullinger likens Cetus to Leviathan, the sea beast (Isaiah 27:1; Job 41). Bullinger notes that Cetus is the natural enemy of fish. These factors have led some to conclude that this area of the heavens represents the "lawless one." Note that three constellations are connected. We can compare the beast from the sea in Cetus (Revelation 13: 1), the second beast out of the earth, the lamb with two horns, in Aries (v. 11) and the image of the Beast in the "head of Satan" (vv. 14, 15). It even contains the mark in the forehead—the X formed by the paths of the two comets on April 11, 1997 (Revelation 13:16).

While these cosmic signs have passed, we must remember that God uses signs to get our attention, often years before the main events occur.

A SIGNAL OF DOOMSDAY?

Jewish oral tradition states that if a comet ever passes through the constellation Orion, the world would be destroyed. After leaving Perseus and passing through the constellation Taurus, the Hale-Bopp comet did just that. It entered the constellation Orion on May 20, 1997 and exited on June 16, 1997.

This means it was in the Orion constellation during the Biblical festival of Shavuot, or Pentecost, on June 11, 1997, an appointed time. This cosmic activity caused some people who read the signs of the times from a Hebraic and Christian perspective to mark this as a major event.

As I studied the path of Hale-Bopp, it appeared to me that the orbit of the comet would take it through or very near the constellation Argo. Argo is considered "the ship."

ARGO: THE SHIP

According to myth, Argo was the ship that carried Jason and the Argonauts on their mystic quest for the Golden Fleece. In his intriguing book, E.W. Bullinger relates that the story of the Argonauts and their ship has its origins in the account of Noah's Ark. Unfortunately, the original meaning was corrupted through Egyptian and Babylonian astrology, which the Bible speaks against (Deuteronomy 4:14-19).

Could it be that this comet, last seen during Noah's day, was going to pass through the constellation representing a ship, whose origins are actually based on the ancient flood account? While reflecting on this question, I was reminded again of the words of Christ: "As it was in the days of Noah, so shall it be in the days of the son of man" (Luke 17:26).

Jesus said that, in the time of Noah and Lot, people were eating, drinking, planning, marrying, and building (Matthew 24:37-38; Luke 17:27-29). Life went on as usual until the day Noah entered the ark and fire rained down on Sodom and Gomorrah. With warnings written in brick and stone and angels entering a city to warn the righteous to get out, almost no one was concerned about what was coming.

This should be the ultimate warning. Do not become so busy that you fail to discern the signs of the times and become overconfident that things will continue as normal. After all, in a day and hour that you think not the Son of Man will come!

CHAPTER 6

GOD IS A DATE SETTER

God reveals the timing of prophetic events

And he said to me, "Do not seal the say-

ings of the prophecy of this book: for the

time is at hand" (Revelation 22:10).

When the time came for Noah to enter the ark, God was precise about the timing of the flood. He extended the date for the deluge by seven days (Genesis 7:4). After the seven days, the door was closed and judgment immediately erupted on the planet. Noah and his family knew the exact amount of time that remained before the flood.

It is interesting to note that God has marked certain days during major prophetic moments throughout Biblical history and has often pinpointed the exact year or time frame in which pivotal prophetic events would unfold. The one mysterious time frame remains the year, month, day and hour of Christ's return.

Throughout the history of Christianity, men have been intrigued with the possibility of breaking the secret code of when Christ will return. This has been done by calculating important prophetic events and adding or subtracting dates and important numbers, as well as using solar and lunar calculations. For 1,900 years, numerous individuals have made predictions as to when the world would end. Some of these people and their projected dates are:

The Person	Prediction Made	Date
Montanu, Prisca & Maximilla	A.D. 156	Near Future
Novatian	4th Century	Near Future
Donatas	4th Century	Near Future
John of Toledo	1186	Near Future
Melchior Hofman	1531	1531
Sabbatai Zevi	1647	1666
Johann Zimmerman	1693	1694
George Rapp	1804	Near Future
William Miller	1839	1843

Henry Adams	1903	1950
Alexander Bedward	1920	Dec. 31, 1920
Herbert Armstrong	1934	1972, 1976
John Strong	1977	October, 1978
Edgar Wisenutt	1987	1988, 1989
Jehovah's Witnesses	Various	1914, 1976, etc.

Clearly, these individuals, while sincere, missed the date of Christ's return, and in some cases, brought a reproach to prophetic teaching and the cause of Christ. Many of the dates selected were based upon certain prophetic passages that have numbers or combinations of numbers, such as Daniel 12:11, Daniel 12:12 or Revelation 12:6. The numbers 1,290, 1,335 and 1,260 were interpreted as days. So, the 1,290 days of Daniel 12:11 became 1,290 years. The same method was employed with the 1,335 days of Daniel 12:12 and the 1,260 days of Revelation 12:6.

Beginning at key moments of prophetic history, such as the birth of Christ, the Crucifixion, and the destruction of the Temple, these years were calculated, giving a projected date of the end of the age. When dates came and went without any manifestation of Christ's return, the "prophets" then recalculated, pointing out they had unwittingly missed an important nugget. When the recalculation passed without results, other excuses followed and the "prophet" fell into the shadows of obscurity, much like other "prophets" before them.

88 REASONS — ONE REASON WHY NOT

During the late 1980's, Edgar Wisenutt wrote a thesis that caused quite a stir. Titled *88 Reasons Why Jesus Will*

Come in 1988, it was distributed widely before the alleged appearance of Christ. I recall preaching that Christ would not return in September of 1988, because too many people were anticipating that date, and the Bible teaches Christ would return "in a day and hour that we think not" (Luke 12:40).

When September of 1988 passed, Wisenutt immediately corrected his error with a second thesis. Allegedly, he had forgotten about the change over from one B.C. to one A.D. on the calendar; therefore, he was off by one year. Years have passed and neither Wisenutt nor his book, have prophetic credibility.

Such miscalculations have scarred the image of the prophetic message and birthed more scoffers than followers of truth. Should we make an attempt to calculate the time of Christ's return, observe and interpret the signs of the times, or simply believe in the "pan theory," which says that "it will all pan out?"

THE SEARCH IS STILL ON

Trying to guess an exact date for the Rapture is a vain effort. Yet, just as the ancient Hebrew prophets searched for the time of the Messiah's first appearance, there are multitudes of believers who are diligently searching the scriptures in an attempt to discern the signs of the times, hoping to answer the question, "When shall these things be and what shall be the sign of Christ's coming and the end of the age?" (Matthew 24:3). Sincere Christians often reprimand curious believers by saying, "No man will know the day nor the hour of Christ's return" (Mathew 25:13). However, informed students of prophecy remind others that "We cannot know the day and hour, but we can discern the times (signs) and the seasons" (1 Thessalonians 5:1).

God is a Date Setter

It comes as a surprise to some when I say, "God is a date setter." There are many examples in Scripture where God would predict a major future event involving Israel and actually reveal the time in the future when the event would come to pass. One reason for this was to prove to His chosen people that He was a God true to His word and not a false deity like what the heathen worshiped. This is why we have several strong examples of God predicting the future and then giving the exact time when the prophecy would come to pass.

Example 1 – The Timing of the Flood

Years before Noah's flood, God indicated He was grieved with His human creation. The hearts of men were wicked continually, and their imaginations ran wild with filthy thoughts (Genesis 6:5). The Bible says:

> And the Lord said, "My Spirit shall not strive with man forever, for he is indeed flesh; yet his days shall be one hundred and twenty years" (Genesis 6:3).

The word man in this passage is *Adam*, which is the common Hebrew word for man. By the time this prophecy was given, the first man, Adam, had already died, so the prophecy does not allude to the original Adam. The second meaning is that *Adam* is a Hebrew word alluding to mankind in general. In other words, mankind's average lifespan would be 120 years. This is the clear meaning when comparing the life span of men before and after the flood. Prior to the flood, Adam lived for 930 years (Genesis 5:5). However, 10 generations after the flood, Abraham only lived for 175 years (Genesis 25:7). Beginning with Shem, we can see how the life span of generations that followed was dramatically reduced:

The Man	Length of life	Reference
Shem	600 years	Genesis 11:10, 11
Arphaxad	483 years	vv. 12, 13
Salah	433 years	vv. 14, 15
Eber	464 years	vv. 16, 17
Peleg	239 years	vv. 18, 19
Reu	239 years	vv. 20, 21
Serug	230 years	vv. 22, 23
Nahor	148 years	vv. 24, 25
Terah	205 years	vv. 26-32
Abraham	175 years	25:7

Not one person listed in the 10 generations after the flood lived to be 120 years old. The average life span of these ten men was 321.6 years. About 430 years after Abraham, Moses wrote Psalms 90:10, which indicates that man's days would be "seventy and by reason of strength eighty." Now, 3,500 years after Moses' revelation in Psalms 90, the average life span for a modern man in the 21st century is about 77 years.

Another interpretation of the statement "man's days shall be one hundred and twenty," could be an allusion to the time remaining for Noah's generation before God would send the flood! We know that Noah was 500 years old when his sons, Shem, Ham, and Japheth were born (Genesis 5:32). Noah was 600 years old the year of the flood (Genesis 7:11). This would indicate that God gave this warning of the length of time that remained about twenty years before the sons of Noah were born, or exactly 120 years before the flood came. This is an early example of a prophetic timeframe being given prior to the actual event occurring.

EXAMPLE 2 - THE TIMING OF ISRAEL'S DELIVERANCE

One of the most fascinating promises given to Israel was revealed to Abraham over 25 years before Isaac was born, and about 70 years before Jacob. The Almighty not only promised Abraham a nation would be birthed through his son, but God also revealed a major event would transpire one day when the nation was young. God explained to Abraham that his descendants would be strangers in a land that was not their own. This prophecy alluded to Israel under Egyptian bondage. God knew the exact number of years Israel would live in Egypt and then be delivered out.

> Then He said to Abram: "Know certainly that your descendants will be strangers in a land that is not theirs, and will serve them, and they will afflict them four hundred years" (Genesis 15:13).

The time frame was ordained and sealed by God as 400 years. Hundreds of years later, during a devastating famine, Jacob took his 11 sons to Egypt where Joseph was second in command (Genesis 42-45). While dwelling in Egypt, Israel grew into a mighty force that threatened the power of the Egyptians (Exodus 1:9-11). Pharaoh made them slaves in order to build treasure cities (Exodus 1:11). As the Hebrews cried out in their affliction, God remembered His covenant with Abraham and sent Moses to lead the nation out of Egypt and back into the Promised Land (Exodus 2:24; 3:10). The famous Exodus occurred after

400 years! Thus, the promise given to Abraham long before the nation existed came to pass!

EXAMPLE 3 - THE TIMING OF JERICHO'S DESTRUCTION

When Israel crossed the Jordan River to inherit the Promised Land, the first city to conquer was the fortified walled stronghold of Jericho. Instructions for the invasion were given by an angel of the Lord, identified as the "Captain of the Lord's Hosts" (Joshua 5:14, 15). The directions were clear and direct:

> And seven priests shall bear seven trumpets of rams' horns before the ark. But the seventh day you shall march around the city seven times, and the priests shall blow the trumpets (Joshua 6:4).

The timing of the battle was set and the victory was guaranteed. The Hebrew army would march for exactly six days, and on the seventh and final day, they would complete their campaign by marching seven times and blowing the ram's horn on the seventh march. The angel instructed them to shout and God would give them the city. Here is another example of God revealing the exact number of days for the conquest of Jericho. The Jericho victory came after Israel celebrated the Passover, and the walls falling occurred near the time of the Feast of First Fruits.

EXAMPLE 4 - THE TIMING OF THE BABYLONIAN CAPTIVITY

Isaiah and Jeremiah began warning Israel of a future invasion by the Babylonian army. God gave the nation of Israel a precise time frame in which they would be taken as captives and remain under the iron hand of the Babylonians in Babylon:

> And this whole land shall be a desolation, and an astonish-
> ment; and these nations shall serve the king of Babylon sev-
> enty years (Jeremiah 25:11, KJV).

The Lord told Jeremiah three times that Israel would remain in Babylon for 70 years, and afterwards God would bring them out (Jeremiah 25:11, 25:12, 29:10). Scripture reveals that Nebuchadnezzar invaded Israel, destroyed the Temple, seized the precious golden vessels and carried the Jews into Babylon.

Years later, in Babylon the prophet Daniel was studying the scroll of Jeremiah and read the prophecy about the 70 years of captivity (Daniel 9:2). This prediction by Jeremiah caused Daniel to begin repenting for Israel's sins and praying for God to fulfill His promise and restore the Jewish nation and Jerusalem. Daniel's prayers were answered. After 70 years, the Hebrew nation came back to the Promised Land!

EXAMPLE 5 - THE DESTRUCTION OF THE SECOND TEMPLE

One of the more startling predictions in the ministry of Christ was that the Temple in Jerusalem would be destroyed a second time (Matthew 24:1-2). The future destruction would be the result of Israel shedding the blood of the righteous prophets God had sent to them, and they had rejected (Matthew 23:33-39). Christ predicted that the trouble (destruction) would come upon this generation!

> Verily I say unto you, all these things shall come upon this
> generation (Matthew 23:36, KJV).

According to Psalms 95:10, a generation of unbelief is a period of 40 years. This is also implied in the fact that Jesus gave His warnings of Jerusalem's destruction around A.D. 30, and the Temple was destroyed in A.D. 70, or 40 years later. When Jesus told the religious un-believers of His day that the judgment of God was com-ing to their generation, this indicated they would have an estimated 40-year period before the actual wrath of God was poured out upon the city.

EXAMPLE 6 - THE TIMING OF THE TRIBULATION

The Bible predicts a time in the future called the Tribu-lation (Matthew 24:21; Revelation 7:14). Ministers often point out that this time period is seven years long. There are several allusions to this seven-year time frame throughout Scripture. One is called Jacob's trouble.

1. JACOB'S TROUBLE

Alas! For that day is great, so that none is like it; and it is the time of Jacob's trouble, but he shall be saved out of it (Jeremiah 30:7).

Jacob's trouble refers to the time when Jacob went to Syria to work for Laban, his mother's brother. Jacob saw one of Laban's beautiful daughters and requested her for his wife. Laban required Jacob to work seven years be-fore he would grant permission for his daughter to marry Jacob (Genesis 29:18-21).

After seven years, Laban tricked Jacob and gave him Leah, his oldest daughter. In order to receive Rachel, Laban told Jacob, "Fulfill her week" (Genesis 29:27). Jacob worked seven additional years to obtain the prize, the woman of his dreams, Rachel. Jacob's trouble was two periods of seven years of intense labor, before he re-ceived his "promise." Some rabbis believe "Jacob's trouble" occurred during the time of the Jewish Holocaust. They note that from 1939, when severe persecution of the Jews began, to the conclusion of the war in 1945 is a period of seven years. Christian scholars note that the future Tribulation (Jacob's trouble) is also seven years. Which interpretation is correct? Both of them could be correct. Jacob had two phases of seven years of Tribulation! The Holocaust was one phase and serves as a preview of the future seven-year time of trouble.

The second prophetic scripture alluding to the seven-year Tribulation in recorded in the prophecy of Daniel's 70 weeks. The final seven years of human government under the Antichrist are alluded to in Daniel 9:27:

> Then he shall confirm a covenant with many for one week; but in the middle of the week he shall bring an end to sacrifice and offering. And on the wing of abominations shall be one who makes desolate, even until the consummation, which is determined, is poured out on the desolate.

In the original Hebrew, the word week is *shabua* and refers to a week of seven years, not seven days. Recent translations of the Bible state he will confirm the covenant with many for "one seven" (*TLB*) or for "seven years" (*NIV*). Notice that in the midst of the week this future leader, the Antichrist, will set up his abomination on the wing of the Temple.

This prophecy is further expounded in Revelation 13, when the False Prophet creates an image of the beast and, through demonic power, causes the image to speak and live (vv. 11-17). This deceptive event happens in the midst of the week, or in the middle of the seven-year Tribulation.

The third reference to the seven-year time frame of the coming Tribulation is found in the Book of Revelation. Chapters 4-22 allude to future events, covering seven years. They are divided into 42 months and 42 months (Revelation 11:2; 13:5). The first 42 months reveal the wrath of the Lamb, and the second 42 months induce the wrath of God (Revelation 6:16, 14:10). Thousands of years ago, the time frame of the final Tribulation was set as seven years. God sets prophetic time frames!

EXAMPLE 7 - THE TIMING OF CHRIST'S REIGN

The final day of the seven-year tribulation will initiate the first day of Christ's rule on the earth in Jerusalem. The length of Christ's rule on earth will be 1,000 years:

> And I saw thrones, and they sat on them, and judgment was committed to them. Then I saw the souls of those who had been beheaded for their witness to Jesus and for the word of God, who had not worshiped the beast or his image, and had not received his mark on their foreheads or on their hands. And they lived and reigned with Christ for a thousand years (Revelation 20:4).

John mentions the 1,000-year reign of Christ six times in Revelation 20:2-7. During this 1,000-year period, Christ will sit on His throne in Jerusalem, and the saints will rule with Him. This age is known as the kingdom of the Messiah. Again, we see that God has set the time in advance.

WHY IS THE CATCHING AWAY HIDDEN?

The above references are clear examples of how certain prophetic events were predicted and given a specific time frame in which to be fulfilled. Why has the Lord hidden the exact day and hour of Christ's return from his own people? The Apostle Paul gives us clues that answer this question.

> Looking for the blessed hope and glorious appearing of our great God and Savior Jesus Christ who gave himself for us, that he might redeem us from every lawless deed and purify for himself his own special people, zealous for good works (Titus 2:13, 14).

The possibility that Christ could return at any moment should cause every believer to live a sober and righteous life. The mystery of His return motivates and encourages a believer to completely follow the Lord.

> Beloved, now are we the sons of God, and it doth not yet appear what we shall be: but we know that, when he shall appear, we shall be like him; for we shall see him as he is. And every man that hath this hope in him purifieth himself, even as he is pure (1 John 3:2, 3, KJV).

The reality of Christ's sudden return causes a believer to purify himself through repentance and prayer. Plan as though Christ may not return for some time, but live as though He may come tomorrow.

> Be ye also patient; establish your hearts: for the coming of the Lord draws near (James 5:8, KJV).

The coming of the Lord should stabilize our relationship with God. Many Christians have an up-and-down seasonal relationship with Christ. They are in church today and out tomorrow. We are told to not forsake the assembling of ourselves together as we see the day of Christ's return approaching (Hebrews 10:25).

THE JEWISH WEDDING

Another reason for the secrecy of the Rapture timing is linked to the ancient Jewish wedding. The actual wedding consisted of two stages. The first part was called the *Erusin* or the *Kiddushin* and was the betrothal or the

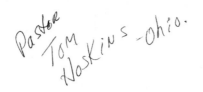
Pastor Tom Hoskins -Ohio.

engagement. The latter was the *Nisu'in*, which was the formal ceremony. In modern culture, an engaged couple may date for several months before the marriage ceremony. In Christ's time, when a couple was engaged, they did not communicate or visit prior to the wedding. The bridegroom prepared a room in his father's house where he and his bride could dwell. The future bride was unaware of the day or the <u>hour</u> when her beloved would return and carry her to their new dwelling place.

Jesus said: "In My Father's house are many mansions . . . I go to prepare a place for you" (John 14:1, 2). Christ said no one knows the day or the hour except the Father. A custom in the ancient wedding gave the groom no control over when he would receive his bride. Once the place was prepared, the father gave the signal that the time to receive the <u>bride had arrived.</u>

The custom of the ancient Jewish wedding is a prophetic picture of Christ and the church. We sit at the Lord's table and partake of His sufferings through the bread and the <u>fruit of the vine (the communion supper</u>), and we are demonstrating our love for Him until He comes. The fact that we are unaware of the time of His coming should spark a fire of excitement in our spirits.

Those who criticize the Rapture teaching often accuse those who believe in this secret catching away of sitting around doing nothing, waiting for Jesus to return. Skeptics who cut the Rapture teaching with such weak arguments have not encountered the hundreds of thousands of believers I have ministered to.

Those who believe Christ could return soon support missions efforts, build Bible schools, and are actively involved in local churches. Those who deny the soon return are actually walking after their own lusts.

CHAPTER 7

THE TIMES OF RESTITUTION

The key to the return of Jesus Christ

Repent therefore and be converted, that your sins may be blotted out, so that times of refreshing may come from the presence of the Lord, and that He may send Jesus Christ, who was preached to you before, whom heaven must receive until the times of restoration of all things, which God has spoken by the mouth of all his holy prophets since the world began (Acts 3:19-21).

The Apostle Peter quoted this passage to a Jewish audience. According to Peter, Christ is now positioned in heaven; and as Paul reveals, Christ is presently serving as the High Priest and Mediator of our faith (Hebrews 8:6). In the future, a season called the "times of restitution," or the "fullness of times" will initiate the release of Christ from heaven and pave the way for His visible return.

Peter indicates that the holy prophets were given insights into these seasons of restitution since the beginning of the world. If we can interpret the meaning of the times of restitution of all things, we will have a fuller understanding of the timing of Christ's return.

The Greek word for "restitution" is *apokatastaseoos*, and only occurs in the New Testament in Acts 3:21. The verb from which the word is derived is found eight times in the New Testament. This verb often alludes to restoring something to its former condition, such as restoring a strained or dislocated limb to its former soundness.

W.E.Vines' *Expository Dictionary of New Testament Words* says there are three possible meanings of the word *restitution*. They are: "to set back in order," "balancing accounts and restoring property to its rightful owner," and according to an Egyptian document, "a consummation of the world's cyclical periods."

The third meaning indicates the ancient belief that the history of the world moves in cycles. The second meaning alludes to returning property to the original owner. According to *Barnes Notes* commentary on Acts 3:2:

> Thus, in Josephus (Antiq., 2:3, 8), the word is used to denote the return of the Jews from the captivity of Babylon, and their restoration to their former state and privileges. The word has also the idea of consummation, completion, or filling up. Thus,

it is used in Philo, Hesychius, Phavorinus, and by the Greek Classics.

The Jews were twice taken from their nation and twice they returned . . . restored back to their homeland. One was 70 years after the Babylonian captivity, and the second time was in 1948, after Israel was restored as a nation. The prophet Isaiah predicted these double returns:

> It shall come to pass in that day that the Lord shall set His hand again the second time to recover the remnant of His people who are left, from Assyria and Egypt, from Pathros and Cush, from Elam and Shinar, from Hamath and the islands of the sea (Isaiah 11:11).

THE TIMES OF RESTITUTION

Peter noted there would be times of restitution. In Acts 3, he speaks about times of refreshing and times of restitution. There are two different Greek words for *times* in this passage. The Greek word for times of refreshing is *kairos*, "a set opportunity." The Greek word for times of restitution is *chronos*, "a space of time, a season."

There are periods of times, or seasons, when the restitution of prophetic things will begin. According to the Hebrew prophets, especially those who penned the Old Testament Scriptures, certain key events will come to pass, thrusting the world into the "seasons of restoration," which will climax in the return of the Messiah. These predicted times of restitution begin to transpire during God-appointed seasons, in a series of phases.

After 26 years of studying prophecy, I am convinced that the restitution began with the re-establishment of the modern state of Israel. This modern miracle did not officially occur until 1948. However, several important events set the stage for this event many years earlier. I call these events the eleventh hour miracle. Before detailing the first phase of the restitution, let us examine the events preceding it.

THE ELEVENTH HOUR MIRACLES

Midnight Hour

Many Jewish teachers believe the Messiah will make His appearance at midnight. Even the Parable of the Ten Virgins indicates the call came at midnight. The bridegroom (a picture of Christ) came at midnight. Events that precede this midnight arrival can be considered the footsteps of the Messiah. Such an event occurred in 1917 that prepared the way for the rebirth of Israel in 1948.

At the outbreak of World War I in 1914, there were 85,000 Jews living in Palestine. At that time, the Turk's Ottoman Empire was in control of Palestine and Jerusalem. At the outbreak of the War, the Turks chose to side with Germany. This forced many Jews to leave the country, reducing their numbers to 56,000. During World War I, a Christian British General named Edmund Allenby led his forces through Egypt and into Palestine. Allenby's faith in God and his understanding of the Scriptures enabled him to march into Palestine. He believed it was the will of God to retake the city of Jerusalem from the Turks. Many amazing stories have been handed down for many years regarding Allenby's faith in retaking Jerusalem.

One such story tells how Allenby, on the outskirts of Jerusalem, was concerned about bloodshed in the Holy City. One evening he opened his Bible and read:

> For thus hath the Lord spoken unto me, Like as the lion and the young lion roaring on his prey, when a multitude of shepherds is called forth against him, he will not be afraid of their voice, nor

abase himself for the noise of them: so shall the Lord of hosts come down to fight for mount Zion, and for the hill thereof.

As birds flying, so will the Lord of hosts defend Jerusalem; defending also He will deliver it; and passing over He will pre- serve it (Isaiah 31:4, 5).

Notice the main points in this prophecy:

- ♦ The deliverer is compared to a lion; the emblem of Britain is a lion.
- ♦ The battle will be over Zion; ancient Zion is the city of Jerusalem.
- ♦ The battle over Jerusalem will be as birds flying; the British had airplanes.
- ♦ As birds flying, Jerusalem would be delivered and preserved.

Allenby instructed that leaflets be printed in the Turk- ish language. They demanded the Turks to surrender Jerusalem.

The story is told that when the scout planes of the delivering forces flew overhead, many of the Turks had never seen an airplane. As they read the leaflets, they misread Allenby's name as Allah-Nebi. *Allah* is the Ara- bic name for *God*, and *Nebi* is the Arabic word for prophet. The Turks surrendered the city without firing a shot! General Allenby entered the city of Jerusalem on December 11, 1917.

World War I ended on November 11, 1918, at 11 o'clock. This was the 11th hour, the 11th day of the month, the 11th month of the year, and 11 months after Allenby entered Jerusalem. The 11th hour precedes the mid- night hour.

But another interesting sign relates to the time frame of Jerusalem being liberated by the British.

THE 1,335 DAYS/YEARS

For centuries Palestine, and especially Jerusalem, have been under the control of the Muslims. The Islamic calendar actually began in the year A.D. 622. Several years later, the Muslims occupied the city and the famous mosques were built on the Temple Mount platform. There was a brief period of time during the Crusades in which Jerusalem was passed back and forth between the Crusaders and the Muslims.

In the Book of Daniel, there is a unique prophecy dealing with a special time frame:

> Blessed is he that waiteth, and cometh to the thousand three hundred and five and thirty days (Daniel 12:12, KJV).

It should be noted that all prophecy could have a primary and a secondary meaning. There is a literal interpretation, and at times there can be a secondary fulfillment. This prediction in Daniel will literally be fulfilled at the return of Christ. However, there is a possibility of a secondary meaning when we take the 1,335 days and make them 1,335 years.

This is what God did to ancient Israel. The spies spent 40 days scoping out the land and returned in unbelief. God said Israel would spend 40 years wandering in the wilderness, a year for every day (Numbers 14:34).

It is interesting to note that from the beginning of the Muslim calendar in 622 to the year 1917 is exactly 1,335 years! In 1917, a Turkish coin was minted with the Islamic year 1335! (I purchased this exact coin from a coin dealer in Jerusalem. See the photo in the center section.) Was this a coincidence? After 1,335 years, the Islamic control over Palestine began to break as the British took control over Palestine. With the British being cordial and friendly to the Jewish people, God was placing the proper leadership in control of the nation to open the door for the rebirth of Israel over 30 years later!

THE 400-YEAR CYCLE

God gave Abraham a direct prediction that his children would be taken into a strange nation for 400 years (Genesis 15:13). After the 400-year time frame was complete, God promised to bring the nation out of the strange land and return them to the land of Abraham. This prophecy was fulfilled as Israel spent 400 years in Egypt and then God delivered the people from Pharaoh's bondage and brought them into the Promised Land.

This 400-year cycle was repeated with the nation of Israel in more modern times. In 1517 A.D., the Turks invaded and captured Egypt and Israel. During their rule over Jerusalem, the Turkish governor in Jerusalem actually rebuilt the walls of the old city, adding a beautiful addition atop the walls. This may have been a partial fulfillment of Isaiah's prophecy:

> The sons of strangers shall build up thy walls, and their kings shall minister unto thee: for in my wrath I smote thee, but in my favor have I had mercy on thee. Therefore thy gates shall be open continually: they shall not be shut day nor night; that men may bring unto thee the forces of the Gentiles (Isaiah 60:10, 11, KJV).

The occupation of Palestine by the British and the deliverance and preservation of Jerusalem by General Allenby in 1917, happened 400 years after the Turks took control of the Promised Land. Just as God brought Israel out of the Egyptian bondage after 400 years, He broke the power of a major Islamic Empire and replaced it with

This salt mountain is located in southern Israel at the Dead Sea, where ancient Sodom was destroyed. (Page 108)

תולדות

Toledot - "generations" of heaven and earth
Genesis 2:4

תולדת

"generations" of Adam
Genesis 5:1

תולדות

"generations" of Pharez . . . and Jesse begat David
Ruth 4:18-22

The Hebrew letter vav is missing after Genesis 2:4, but is restored in Ruth 4:18-22. (Page 98)

Salt from Sodom on display at the Temple Institute in Jerusalem.
(Page 108)

1997 - 1998 (5758)
"The Season of Noah (Rest)"

ה׳תשנ״ח

ה - "ha" (the)

ת - "tekufah" (season)

ש - "shel" (of)

נח - "noah" (rest)

The Jewish year 1998 was 5758 on the Hebrew calendar.
When translated into the Hebrew alphabet,
the year forms an acrostic for "The Seasons of Noah." (Page 113)

Year Noah Received Instruction To Build the Ark
The Hebrew Year 1558
א'תקנ"ח

את *et* "Word of God"

קנח *kinach* "to wipe clean"

The Hebrew year that Noah began building the Ark was 1558, which means, "to wipe clean." (Page 113)

The date opposite 1917 is the Arabic for 1335.

١	٢	٣	٤	٥	٦	٧	٨	٩	٠
1	2	3	4	5	6	7	8	9	0

This Turkish coin was minted in 1917,
the 1,335th year of the Islamic calendar. (Page 139)

Just as Isaiah predicted, water is bursting forth in the desert. (Page 148)

This is the pool of water found underground in the Arabah.
Huge farms now use this water for irrigation.

We arrived in Israel during an excavation of "secret chambers."
We held ancient catapult stones once used to destroy Jerusalem
in 70 AD. (Page 127)

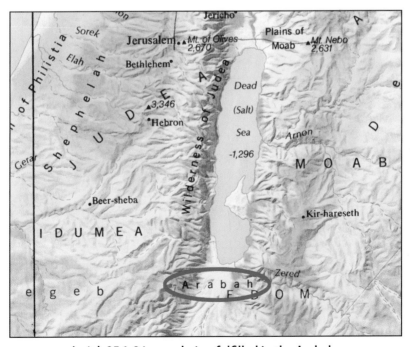

Isaiah 35:1-8 is now being fulfilled in the Arabah,
a desolate area south of the Dead Sea. (Page 148)

These are bricks from the ancient wall of Jericho.
Rahab's house survived "on the wall." (Page 125)

An example of an ancient oil lamp, made of clay. (Page 201)

One of forty pieces of pottery containing the "Messianic Seal" discovered in the grotto on Mount Zion. (Page 152)

A tunnel cut out by hand connects two large rooms (cisterns) in the grotto where Teek Oteeos found the Messianic Seal pottery.

Jesus said that two would be grinding at the mill—one would be taken, the other left. Primitive nations still use grinding mills and olive presses. (Page 203)

This is the area of northern Israel known as the Bashan, or Golan Heights, where the war with Gog and Magog will occur. (Page 49)

The Kidron Valley, just below the Eastern Gate,
is where the judgment of the nations will occur! (Page 222)

These are the ancient ruins of Megiddo, with the
"Valley of Armageddon" in the background. (Page 216)

the Christian British, many of whom were aware of God's end-time plan for the Hebrew people. It would take another major war, World War II, to birth the nation of Israel. This birthing of Israel was phase one of the restitution of all things!

RESTORATION PHASE ONE

Phase one of the restoration began with the rebirth of Israel as a nation. From the year A.D. 70 to 1948, Israel did not exist as a Jewish nation. In A.D. 70, the 10th Roman legion invaded Jerusalem, burned the Holy Temple, battered the walls to the ground, and took enormous amounts of Jewish prisoners into foreign lands. For centuries the Jews were called "wandering Jews," as they were persecuted and driven from place to place through 1,900 years of history.

In the Tel-Aviv Museum, the provisional leaders of a new Israel met secretly to declare that the state of Israel would come into existence at 12:01 a.m. on May 15, 1948. The British mandate over Palestine would end on May 14. The United Nations had voted to partition Palestine, which allowed the Jews who survived the holocaust to return to their ancient homeland.

When David Ben-Gurion stood in Tel Aviv and read a declaration introducing the new land as the State of Israel, the Hebrew prophets must have rejoiced in paradise. This was the first phase of a series of importations and restorations that must occur prior to the return of the Messiah. Some believe the prophet Isaiah alluded to this event when he wrote:

> Who has heard such a thing? Who has seen such things?
> Shall the earth be made to give birth in one day? Or shall a

nation be born at once? For as soon as Zion was in labor, she gave birth to her children (Isaiah 66:8).

Seven Nations

When ancient Israel finally entered the Promised Land, there were seven nations (tribes) dwelling in the land that Israel had to deal with (Deuteronomy 7:1). When Israel was declared an independent nation on May 15, 1948, they were immediately opposed by seven surrounding nations: Jordan, Syria, Lebanon, Iraq, Saudi Arabia, Yemen and Egypt.

Just as ancient Israel had to continually fight opposition from seven nations to ensure their survival, Israel has had to fight seven Arabic/Islamic nations in order to maintain their survival. Modern Israel has fought five wars, beginning with the War of Independence in 1948, then again in 1956, 1967, 1973, and in Lebanon in 1981. In each conflict, Israel was victorious, often in a miraculous manner.

Restoration Phase Two

The second major phase of the restitution occurred 19 years after phase one. Although Israel was once again a nation among the nations, the holy city of Jerusalem was divided between the nation of Jordan on the east and Israel on the west. A huge concrete barrier with rolls of barbed wire separated the Arabs and Jews, the Jordanians and the Israelis, in the ancient city.

Few Jews ever imagined that in their lifetimes a brief, but fierce, six-day war would reunite the divided halves into one city under total Israeli control. The now-famous

Six-Day War returned Jerusalem to Jewish hands on the third day of the war. On June 7, at 10 o'clock in the morning, the Israeli military made the announcement that the "city is in our hands." Word soon spread, and thousands of Israelis ran toward the western wall shouting, rejoicing, weeping and celebrating.

Immediately, the concrete barriers were abolished and the barbed wire was destroyed. Jerusalem was reunified as the capital of Israel.

The restoration of Israel and the reunification of Jerusalem have not gone without conflict with the Islamic nations. Since Israel (called Palestine by the Arabs and Muslims) was once in the possession of Muslims, the Islamic belief is that it is now in the hands of infidels and must be liberated by political pressure or by Jihad.

The centerpiece of Jerusalem is the famous Islamic mosque, the Dome of the Rock, whose gold plated dome towers above all other buildings in the area. This dome and the land surrounding it comprise the most controversial and volatile property on the planet.

Since 1948, especially since 1967, Muslims have made Jerusalem the third holiest city in Islam. Fanatical Muslims have demanded the removal of all Jewish and Christian presence from Jerusalem. This controversy was predicted thousands of years ago by the prophet Zechariah, when God announced:

> Behold, I will make Jerusalem a cup of drunkenness to all the surrounding peoples, when they lay siege against Judah and Jerusalem. And it shall happen in that day that I will make Jerusalem a very heavy stone for all peoples; all who would heave it away will surely be cut in pieces, though all nations of the earth are gathered against it (Zechariah 12:2, 3).

Despite the controversy over Jerusalem, Jewish immigrants continue to pour into Israel from the nations of the earth. It is still the Jewish capital of Israel and the city continues to grow. The surge in Jewish immigrants returning to their spiritual roots brings to mind a powerful prophecy: "When the Lord shall build up Zion, he will appear in his glory" (Psalms 102:16, KJV). The restoration of Israel and the reunification of Jerusalem are two major phases of the restitution of all things, spoken of by the prophets.

RESTORATION PHASE THREE

For centuries, Hebrew prophets predicted that the Jews would be scattered throughout the nations and return at the end of days. This return of the Jews back to their homeland is phase three of the restoration (restitution) process.

At the turn of the century, the Jewish people had established themselves as bankers and prominent business owners in much of Europe, and especially in Germany, Austria and Eastern Europe. Just as were their ancestors before them who once settled in Egypt, the Jews were happy and content living outside their promised homeland until severe persecution fell upon them.

In days of old, the Hebrew nation lived in Egypt for 400 years. Eventually a cruel Pharaoh rose to the throne who felt threatened by the Hebrew nation. Under his command, the male children were killed at birth and the adults were brought under military control and eventual slavery (Exodus 1:8-12). When they cried out to God, the Lord "remembered His covenant" and began a plan for their release and return to the Promised Land (Exodus 2:24).

A modern Pharaoh named Adolph Hitler instigated the violent persecution against the Jews of Europe. This cruel tyrant was the leader of the Third Reich, also known as the Nazi Party. Hitler demonically mesmerized the masses and initiated the final solution to rid the world of all Jews.

During seven years of horror called the Holocaust, six million Jews perished in the death camps and torture chambers of the Nazis. The cries of Jews were heard in heaven, just as they were at the time of the Egyptian captivity.

God brought both generations of Hebrews out of their bondage through a massive Exodus, and both generations witnessed the destruction of both Pharaohs and their armies. The Exodus from Egypt and the Exodus from Europe opened the door for a remnant of Jews to return to their promised homeland. Biblical prophets predicted the Jews would return from the four points of the compass, namely the north, south, east and west.

> Fear not, for I am with you; I will bring your descendants from the east, and gather you from the west; I will say to the north, "Give them up," and to the south, "Do not keep them back!" Bring My sons from afar, and My daughters from the ends of the earth (Isaiah 43:5, 6).

The re-establishment of Israel as a nation in 1948 seemed to cause Jews from various nations to develop a renewed interest in returning to the land of their fathers. Persecution against Jews began breaking out in Arab nations once tolerant toward the Hebrew spiritual heritage and beliefs. Synagogues were attacked. Frustrated Muslims, angered over Israel's rebirth, mobbed Jews. The social, political and religious pressure forced the Jews into their new homeland in droves.

In September 1950, over 50,000 Jews were airlifted from Yemen in a project called Operation Flying Carpet. A second wave of Jewish immigrants returned in July 1951 from Iraq. Over 122,000 Jews claimed to be direct descendants of the Jews who lived in Babylon. Between November 1984 and March 1985, more than 8,000 Jews returned from Ethiopia.

This massive return of the Jews was made possible through modern transportation—the airplane. This phenomenon may be alluded to in some strange prophecies:

> These shall come from afar; look! Those from the north and the west, and these from the land of Sinim (Isaiah 49:12).

> Lift up your eyes all around, and see: they all gather together, they come to you; your sons shall come from afar, and your daughters shall be nursed at your side (Isaiah 60:4).

> Who are these that fly as a cloud, and as the doves to their windows? (Isaiah 60:8, KJV).

The American Zionist Council reported in 1950, "The children of Israel are returning from the furthest corners of their exile and flying as a cloud in airplanes." Jews returned from Iran, Iraq, Egypt, Libya, Syria, Lebanon and Ethiopia.

By the late 1980s, the new freedom in Russia opened doors for a massive Exodus back to Israel. The prophet Jeremiah predicted this return, called Exodus II by some Christians.

> Behold, I will bring them from the north country, and gather them from the ends of the earth, among them the blind and the lame, the woman with child and the one who labors with child, together; a great throng shall return there (Jeremiah 31:8).

The return of Jews from the four winds of the earth continues to the present day. Recently, the prime minister of Israel announced his desire to see a million Jews return from the Gentile nations and become permanent residents in Israel.

RESTORATION PHASE FOUR

Phase four is obvious when a person travels the length and breadth of modern Israel, which I have done on over 22 occasions. One of the ancient rabbinical signs indicating the Messiah will soon return and set up His rule from Jerusalem is when the land of Israel begins to blossom and fill the world with fruit.

Prior to 1948, this land called Palestine was either dry and desolate or a swamp. Entire sections of the country were unable to produce any form of vegetation or sustain life.

One such remote region was the arid wilderness called the Arabah. Often identified as "God-forsaken" by many Israelis, one section of this area begins south of the Dead Sea and continues for 120 miles south to the Gulf Of Aquabah. The width is from 8-20 miles, stretching from Israel on the west bank to Jordan on the east bank.

Since the beginning of time, no edible produce has grown in this area. The only vegetation has been a few frail shrubs and some Acacia trees, known for surviving in arid deserts. Twenty-five centuries ago, the prophet Isaiah caught a vision of God's blessing that would come on the land of Israel in the latter days.

> The wilderness and the wasteland shall be glad for them, and the desert shall rejoice and blossom as the rose; it shall blossom abundantly and rejoice, even with joy and singing. The glory of Lebanon shall be given to it, the excellence of Carmel and Sharon. They shall see the glory of the Lord, and the excellency of our God (Isaiah 35:1, 2).

> The parched ground shall become a pool, and the thirsty
> land springs of water; in the habitation of jackals, where each
> lay. There shall be grass with reeds and rushes (Isaiah 35:7).

Eight Hebrew words in the Hebrew Bible are translated *wilderness* or *desert* in our English Bible. Each specifies a geographical location in the land of Israel. There is the word *Sinai,* the word *Negev,* the word *Midbar,* and so forth. The Hebrew word in Isaiah 35:1, used for "desert," is *Arabah.* The location of the Arabah is the region previously described south of the Dead Sea where no fruit or vegetation has ever grown. No known water source to irrigate the parched ground has been available for centuries.

The situation changed over 24 years ago when a satellite image revealed a huge pocket of underground water in the heart of the Arabah. The pressure from the source was already breaking through areas of the desert, and shooting up small streams of water into the air. Israelis drilled down just 1,500 feet and dug a huge opening in the ground, creating a pool of water. Today, this natural water source lies in a beautiful pool of water, called Sapphire, in the heart of the Arabah.

I have visited this site five times, and can attest not only to its existence but to the fact that this underground water source is now responsible for providing water to over forty farms in the heart of the Arabah! (*For complete documentation, see our video* "Israel, Racing Toward the Second Coming.")

Isaiah said there would be "grass, reeds and rushes." All three of these items surround the huge pool of water in the Arabah. The discovery of this water has transformed the desert, and caused it to "blossom as a rose."

It has made possible the fulfillment of another prophecy by Isaiah, which said, "He will cause them that come of Jacob to take root: Israel will blossom and bud, and fill the face of the world with fruit" (Isaiah 27:6). The Hebrew word for fruit in this passage is *tenuwbah*, and is more than apples, oranges and bananas. The word is a general word for *produce*, alluding to all sorts of produce grown for human consumption.

Farms located in the Arabah region are producing tomatoes, green peppers, melons, and a variety of fresh vegetables. Israel has a large company that annually exports thousands of tons of food from the Arabah to nations throughout the world.

This prophecy could not have been fulfilled until Israel was restored as a nation. One of the oral traditions handed down for generations that indicates the Messiah will return is when the desert begins to blossom. Certainly, this is a sign and a blessing to those living in the Promised Land.

RESTORATION PHASE FIVE

I believe another phase to this restoration is often overlooked and underappreciated by the traditional Christian church. The first Christians were Jews, and eventually the Gentiles were grafted into the covenant, beginning with an Italian centurion named Cornelius (Acts 10:1-40). The two groups, Jews and Gentiles, had cultural and religious traditions that immediately created rifts and fractions among them, even in the first century church.

One division stemmed from the concept of circumcision. Jews demanded circumcision as a visible sign of one's covenant with God; however, the Gentiles made no such demands. Some Jewish believers felt that a Gentile was not really saved unless he was circumcised (Acts 11:1-3).

These rifts continued to separate the Gentile church from many wonderful Jewish customs and traditions, such as understanding the Hebrew Feasts. By the fourth century, the Gentile church had become a church controlled by Roman leaders. Latin thinkers covered up the Jewish foundation, and the Greek-Roman culture overtook the Jewish understanding of the Messiah.

For over 14 centuries, the traditional Roman Christian church knew nothing about the Jewish customs, teachings, feasts, and other important Hebraic truths that pointed to Christ's redemption and His future Kingdom. Shortly after 1967, the Charismatic movement began spreading throughout North America.

This movement brought a fresh concept of worship and renewal to the body of Christ (Ephesians 4:11). The teaching ministry began to dig deeper into the truths of God, and began to restore Biblical revelation that was overlooked and seldom taught. Through this restoration of truth, a new understanding and appreciation for our Hebraic roots began emerging.

My personal interest in our Hebraic roots began with my first trip to Israel in 1985. One hundred and twenty Americans traveled in our group as we toured, explored and discovered the land of the Bible. I began to hear teaching of how the New Testament actually demonstrates the fulfillment of the Old Testament prophecies.

I saw my first synagogue and prayer shawls, and discovered many customs and traditions that Jesus and His disciples were familiar with. I realized the seven feasts of Israel were prophetic pictures of future events. I returned to America and began studying the Bible from a Hebraic perspective. Almost immediately, many ministers tagged me as an oddball or a fanatic.

I was accused of trying to bring people back under Judaism. Some said I was returning to "Old Testament stuff." I ignored the critics and continued to enjoy the study of my roots. Today, hundreds of thousands are enjoying the fruit of those studies as the eyes of their understanding have been opened (Ephesians 1:18).

Part of the restoration is for the body of Christ to have their Hebrew heritage restored. Since 1967, the Gentile church has been re-introduced to the original trumpet— the ram's horn or shofar. A fresh understanding of the seven feasts of the Lord has led to a greater appreciation for our heritage and greater love for the Hebrew people and the nation of Israel.

Our own ministry has been actively researching, teaching, and preaching the Hebraic roots of Christianity. I personally believe this is one of several reasons why the blessings of the Lord have followed our ministry for so many years.

RESTORING RELATIONSHIPS

During the first century, Peter was the apostle to the Jewish branch of the church, and Paul was the apostle to the Gentile branch of the church. Both the Jewish and Gentile believers were united under Christ. After centuries of religious bickering and division, there is now a bridge being built between the evangelical Christians in North America and the Jewish people, especially in Israel.

An unusual discovery following the 1967 War may reveal how God is attempting to bridge the Jews and Gentiles again. The following excerpts are taken from my book *Plucking the Eagle's Wings*.

Pottery on Mount Zion

An item described as the "Messianic Seal of the Jerusalem Church" was discovered on several pieces of first century pottery in Jerusalem. Reuven Schmaltz and Raymond Fisher have released the information about this seal in a book called *The Messianic Seal of the Jerusalem Church.* The 97-page book, printed by Olim Publications in Tiberias, Israel, gives the account of a meeting between the authors and Ludwig Schneider, a German living in Israel.

According to the book, in 1990, Mr. Schneider befriended a lone monk who was living in a small building in the Old City of Jerusalem. After the third visit, the monk, a Greek named Teek Oteeoos, invited Ludwig into his small, musty dwelling to show him a discovery he had made in 1969 in the area of Mount Zion. According to Greek tradition, this area was the location of the first church in Jerusalem, pastored by James. To Ludwig's amazement, the monk had about 40 pieces of pottery, including an oil lamp, clay jars, and other first century vessels that he had unearthed in an old grotto on property not far from the tomb of David.

It was not the pottery that struck Ludwig, but a strange emblem that was either etched or painted on all the pottery pieces. The emblem appeared to be a Jewish seven branched menorah drawn with a triangular base, with the triangular tail of a small fish overlapping the bottom half of the menorah. The triangular base of the menorah and the triangular tail of the fish intersected to form a Star of David, the emblem of Israel that appears on the national flag. (See the photo in the center section).

The monk eventually gave Ludwig eight pieces of this unusual pottery with this unique design. Ludwig now believes this emblem was the Messianic seal of the first century church in Jerusalem. In fact, one large stone block that was unearthed contains the words "for the oil of the spirit." It may have been used to hold a large jar of oil, used to anoint believers.

According to the Bible, James was the leader of the first church in Jerusalem. While the apostle Peter served the Jewish sect of the first church and Paul was chosen as the voice to the Gentile believers, it was James in Acts 15:15 who spoke of God "restoring the tabernacle of David and healing the breach." James also mentioned anointing the sick with oil in the "name of the Lord" (James 5:14).

Could this discovery be evidence of an emblem from the first Christian church that has been hidden for over 1,900 years? In December of 1999, after our Israel tour group departed, Dr. Joe Van Koevering and I extended our stay to tape programs for the January, 2000, episodes of "God's News Behind the News." During our stay, we asked our tour guide, Gideon Shor, if he was familiar with the location of this ancient underground grotto. Gideon knew the location and we were able to visit the grotto that contained the pottery.

On Wednesday, December 5, our camera crews and the three of us went to the actual grotto, which is about 75 yards from the tomb of King David. There is a concrete building and metal cage that surrounds the underground chamber, which also has double metal doors that are chained tight. After making contact with a young man who was a teacher at the Greek school, we were permitted to go inside the grotto and take photographs.

As our Greek guide unlocked the doors and took us down the stone steps, we began to ask him certain questions. He told us the grotto, which is cut out of limestone, was a cistern and appears to have been a Jewish *mikvot*. The *mikvot* was an ancient baptismal pool where the Jews would submerge and purify themselves in water. We walked through a small opening into another room, round in shape and cut from the limestone rock. A small tunnel about 20 feet long led into another room, which was also a large cistern. The monk told us that the entire hill has tunnels under it that branch out, similar to the catacombs under Rome, Italy. The tunnels have been sealed up or filled with debris and are no longer accessible, at least from the area of the ancient grotto.

According to the young teacher who gave us the tour, Helena (the mother of Constantine), came to the Holy Land over 1,600 years ago and built a church on the same hill where these underground tunnels are located. In fact, our guide allowed us to visit the basement of the school and view two sections of a small, mosaic floor that are the only remaining pieces of evidence from the church of Helena, built on the land where some believe the early Christians met in secret.

Our guide was not familiar with the story of Teek Oteeoos, or the discovery of the pottery and the ancient seal. The discovery was made years before he became a part of the school. He told us about people we could talk to who may give information if they chose to do so. After years of traveling to Israel we have discovered it is difficult, if not impossible, to obtain inside information if you are not a part of the particular religious group you are dealing with.

According to Ludwig, the old monk who found the pottery was in his 90s when he gave the special gift of eight pieces of pottery to Ludwig. The monk, Teek Oteeoos, passed away and the remaining pottery was removed from the small building, along with the deceased monk's possessions. Some believe the Greek monastery, which refuses to discuss the subject, may have taken the pottery. Fortunately, Ludwig has visible evidence of the discovery and the seal in his possession.

Gideon Shor was shown a picture of a small stone block with the letters carved on the front. Gideon confirmed that the letters were the old Hebrew letters that would have been used from the first century. Reading right to left, the two words are "Shemon Ruach," or the "oil of the Spirit." The old Hebrew was used until about the fifth century, then the form of the letters changed. The church in Jerusalem was a Jewish church and was pastored by Jewish leaders and elders. So, the language used would have been Hebrew.

In 1996, Ludwig opened a gift shop in the old city and began to make copies of the emblem he believed was the "Messianic Seal of the Jerusalem Church." When certain orthodox Jews became angry over the seal, they began to stone his shop and he was soon forced to close it down. It seems the problem comes from what appears to be a Star of David that is formed when the base of the menorah intersects with the tail of the fish. The Star of David can be traced as far back as the 7th

Century B.C., and is presently the emblem of the nation of Israel. It appears on Israel's national flag.

By placing the menorah (a Jewish emblem) and the fish (an early Christian sign) together, few people would be upset. But on each piece of pottery, the menorah and fish seem to create the image of a Star of David. Prophetically speaking, the menorah was the emblem of the Old Covenant, and the fish was the emblem of the New Covenant. In fact, when Christians were being martyred in Rome, one would draw half of the fish in the sand and the other Christian would draw the other half, thus forming the fish sign.

Evidence indicates an emblem (seal) of the early church may have been found! Some people in Israel have attempted to discredit this discovery. Yet, the seal remains, and has become a popular symbol for Christian jewelry, demonstrating how the breach between Jewish believers and Gentile Christians is being healed!

It is unique that when the menorah, symbolizing the old covenant, and the fish, symbolizing the new covenant, are placed together, they form the Star of David, which symbolizes Israel. The star on the pottery is the connection between the two covenants. In the same way, modern Israel is the prophetic bridge that helps us understand end-time prophecy.

I have often said that when Christ returns to rule on earth, He will rule from Jerusalem and not Washington, Brussels or Rome. Christ had a Jewish mother (Mary). He was accustomed to the Torah and the Hebraic teachings, services and customs. It is important to understand that part of this restoration in Hebraic roots is to prepare the body of Christ to rule with Christ during the 1,000 year reign mentioned in Revelation 20:4.

I believe that God is preparing His church for that event now.

Acceleration, Then Accumulation

From A.D. 70 until about 1896, few, if any, ancient prophecies alluding to the return of Christ were fulfilled. Since that time, a slow progression of events began to unfold, which scholars noted was a fulfillment of certain prophecies. However, since 1948, a series of events has been accumulated that create an acceleration of the many end-time predictions of the Biblical prophets.

Even with this proliferation of visible evidence, many people still believe the return of Christ could be hundreds of years from today. Is there ample evidence that the Second Coming could be in the near future? This question is asked and pondered by multitudes of believers. There are 10 reasons I believe we might very well be the generation who will usher in the appearance of the Messiah. These 10 reasons will help you understand why we must certainly be in the time of the end.

CHAPTER 8

TEN SIGNS OF THE TIME OF THE END

Is this the end of the world?

Now as He sat on the Mount of Olives, the

disciples came to Him privately, saying,

"Tell us, when will these things be? And

what will be the sign of Your coming, and

of the end of the world?" (Matthew 24:3).

*C*onfusion exists in the secular world and the Body of Christ regarding the terms used in Scripture and behind pulpits related to the time of the end, or as some have identified it, the end of time. There is also a lack of understanding as to what will actually happen at the conclusion of the age.

This was visible prior to the year 2000. People were buying bottled water by the case. The basic necessities such as bread, milk, and canned goods were flying off the grocery shelves. Local banks saw a huge increase of cash withdrawals from personal savings accounts. Generator sales were on the rise and the sales of personal firearms were breaking records. Some believed this event could initiate the end of modern civilization as we know it. The event was the now-forgotten year 2000 (Y2K) computer glitch.

Prior to the year 2000, the cover of one national news magazine portrayed New York City's local residents as frozen in fear. Leading the charge of prognosticators was a long-haired, shabbily groomed, self-proclaimed prophet of doom dressed in a traditional long white robe and carrying a sign around his neck that announced, "The End of the World is Near." Of course, the end of the world never came, and, to the surprise of many, the end of the world as revealed in the Bible will not actually be the end of the world.

Isn't the World Going to End?

One statement in Mathew 24 has been a cause of debate for centuries. The disciples asked Christ, "What shall be the sign of thy coming and of the end of the world?" (Matthew 24:3, KJV). When the dreaded Tribulation sweeps the earth, weapons of mass destruction will be unleashed and famine will devastate the food supply. Some Christians believe the world will be exterminated and only a small core of humans will survive by storing up tribulation food and building bunkers in remote mountains.

Actually, this misconception can be clarified by examining the words *end* and *world* in Matthew 24:3. The New Testament was originally written in the common Greek language of that day. However, the English translation of the Bible may use a single English word that had three of four various meanings in the original Greek language. So you have to decide by the context of its use which meaning is proper.

For example, if I say *power*, what do you imagine? In the English translation of Scriptures, we use the word *power*. In the Greek text, however, there are two different Greek words. One word for power, *dunamis*, is translated as power in Acts 1:8 and means "miraculous power." Another Greek word for power, *exhousia*, is translated as power in Luke 10:19, and means "spiritual authority." In the English translation, the single word *power* is used for two Greek words that have two different meanings.

The same is true with the word *world*. In English, when we read the word *world*, we visualize the physical planet on which mankind lives. However, in Matthew 24 the word *world* is mentioned three times, and in each case, the Greek meaning has a different connotation.

THREE MEANINGS FOR THE WORD *WORLD*

And this gospel of the kingdom shall be preached in all the world for a witness unto all nations; and then shall the end come (v. 14, KJV).

The Greek word for *world* in this passage is *oikoumene,* which in Christ's time was primarily the region of the Roman Empire and was the known civilized world at that time.

> For then shall be great tribulation, such as was not since the beginning of the world to this time, no, nor ever shall be (Matthew 24:21, KJV)

The Greek word for world in the above verse is *kosmos,* and alludes more to the human beings who dwell on the earth. We could say, "There shall be a tribulation unlike any since the beginning of humanity." The third reference reads:

> And as he sat upon the mount of Olives, the disciples came to him privately, saying, Tell us, when shall these things be? And what shall be the sign of thy coming, and of the end of the world? (v. 3, KJV).

The King James translation speaks of the "end of the world." The Greek word for world in this passage is *aion,* and alludes to "the age." The disciples were asking about the signs of Christ's coming and the "end of the age," not the physical destruction of the planet. To the disciples, the end of the age would prophetically be the age (*aion*) climaxing with the termination of the Roman occupation in Israel and the setting up of Messiah's kingdom on the earth (Acts 1:6).

The concept of the termination of the world has been misrepresented in some prophetic circles. Yes, the coming Tribulation will be an environmental nightmare as a third of the trees and grass are burned and a third of the water supply becomes undrinkable (Revelation 8:7 and 8:11). Yet, the end of the world (the age of human government) will conclude on the day that Christ returns to earth to reign for 1,000 years (Revelation 20:4). On that day, the kingdoms of the world will become the kingdoms of our God (Revelation 11:15). The end of the world is actually the conclusion of human government and the beginning of Christ's kingdom.

It is also important to examine the Greek word for *end* in the phrase "end of the world" (Matthew 24:3). The word is *sunteleia* and means "completion, or the consummation of a dispensation of time." According to the Apostle Paul's revelation, mankind is presently living in the time of the Gentiles, when the grace of God has been extended to the Gentile nations and the gospel of Christ is being proclaimed among the nations (Romans 1:5). When the gospel is preached as a witness to all nations, then the end comes.

> And this gospel of the kingdom will be preached in all the world as a witness to all nations; and then the end will come (Matthew 24:14).

For the church age, identified as the "dispensation of the grace of God" Ephesians 3:2), the end will arrive the moment Christ returns to gather His church and resurrect the dead in Christ.

> That in the dispensation of the fullness of the times He might gather together in one all things in Christ, both which are in heaven and which are on earth—in Him (Ephesians 1:10).

The end is not actually the end as we think of it. It is literally a change in the governmental order and structure among the nations.

STEPPING STONES AND MILESTONES

A stepping stone takes you to another level. A milestone is a marker that indicates a definite point of time or distance. There are prophetic stepping stones and prophetic milestones. A prophetic milestone is an incident that is a direct fulfillment of prophecy. A stepping stone is an event that leads to a milestone. The birth of Christ was a milestone, predicted by Old Testament prophets. The Messiah was to be born of a virgin (Isaiah 7:14), in the city of Bethlehem (Micah 5:2), with the sign of a star appearing over Israel (Numbers 24:17). Christ fulfilled these prophetic expectations; therefore, His birth was a prophetic milestone.

Prophet Isaiah foretold the death of Christ over 600 years before the event. Isaiah saw Him despised and rejected of men (Isaiah 53:3). Isaiah said He would be made a sin offering, be beaten for our healing and be buried in a rich man's grave (Isaiah 53:4-10). From the time of Christ's arrest until His burial in the tomb, He fulfilled the expectations of Isaiah's suffering servant! His death and resurrection were prophetic milestones.

In modern times, the restoration of Israel as a nation, the reunification of Jerusalem, and the return of the Jews to their homeland are all prophetic milestones. There are often more stepping stones than there are milestones. A combination of stepping stones leads to the milestones. For example, the Holocaust was a horrible nightmare to the Jewish population. Yet, it was the stepping stone that led to the re-establishment of Israel as a modern nation. The Gentile nations had pity on the Jews who survived the Holocaust, and this compassion moved them to accept the Jewish state.

The fall of the Berlin Wall and the collapse of the Iron Curtain in the Soviet Union were not directly foretold in Scripture. However, these two events were keys that opened the door for the oppressed Jews in communist-controlled nations to obtain visas and immigrate back to the land of their ancient fathers. The fall of communism was a stepping stone, but the return of the Jews is a milestone predicted by numerous Hebrew prophets.

No verse in the Bible specifically gave America a warning of the September 11th terrorist attacks. Nor did a single passage predict the results of the war in Iraq. When such events with wide-ranging global impact strike the earth, we must remember that the initial event may be a stepping stone leading to the direct fulfillment of ancient prophecies.

IS IT REALLY THE TIME OF THE END?

After many years of full-time ministry, I have made some simple, yet important, observations and discoveries. The first observation is that interest in Biblical prophecy and future events according to the Bible runs in cycles. Human interest is comparable to the cycle on your washing machine—it moves from hot to cold in a short time.

Months before the Y2K computer scare, prophetic conferences were crowded with Americans concerned about whether their microwaves would heat their frozen dinners and their toilets would flush on January 1, 2000. Soon the fears subsided, however. The anxiety ceased, and the additional food supplies were devoured in a month. The same type of response immediately followed the terrorist attacks of September 11. The following day, I was occupied with four telephone interviews; the next day was I was on a four-hour live television special in Atlanta, Georgia.

The Sunday after the terrorist attacks, church attendance was up 30 percent from coast to coast. Within four weeks, it was back to normal and, in some churches, the national average dropped for the month of November.

The war with Iraq created a media feeding frenzy. The possibility of a chemical or biological attack sent chills up our spines. The predictions were out as the prognosticators analyzed the coming clash between the oldest nation on earth and one of the youngest on earth. Some suggested over 50,000 Americans would perish, and the city of Baghdad would be scorched into oblivion with a nuclear or biological weapon.

Two months before the battle, large crowds packed the churches where I was preaching. I boldly told one group, "You'll be here as long as you don't know what is going to happen, but I won't see many of you when the war is over."

How did I know? I have witnessed this high interest in prophecy during uncertain times on five occasions in the past 26 years. Curiosity in Biblical prophecy is seasonal. This is because many say they believe we are in the time of the end, but the majority are totally uncertain.

The question is, "Are we, or are we not, in the time of the end?" I want to suggest 10 reasons I believe we are in the time of the end. These observations are not prophetic milestones, but are a series of stepping stones that will eventually open the door to fulfill the Biblical prophecies related to Christ's return.

1. DESTRUCTIVE WEAPONS IN THE WRONG HANDS

But know this, that in the last days perilous times will come (2 Timothy 3:1).

The word *perilous* in this verse means "fierce or dangerous." It carries the idea of reducing the strength. The main purpose of the war in Iraq was to stop Saddam from manufacturing chemical and biological weapons. He could place deadly chemical materials into the hands of terrorists who would, in turn, sneak them into America.

Our nation saw firsthand what effects one teaspoon of anthrax in a small envelope had on the postal service and the Senate building in Washington. According to reports, Saddam produced thousands of gallons of anthrax that were never accounted for by United Nations inspectors.

Small terrorist cells arrested in London have already been accused of processing ricin, a chemical so deadly that if released, people would die within minutes. The fact that massive casualties could result from one major biological attack is one indicator of the perilous times Paul warned Timothy about. According to my sources, it is only a matter of time before terrorists strike a heavy blow to a major American city. One military intelligence person told me, "It is not *if* an attack happens, but *when* it happens."

Terrorist cells, called sleeper cells, lurk quietly in the shadows, undetected. They will wait patiently until America feels secure again and activities appear to be back to normal. Then suddenly, like a venomous viper camouflaged by its surroundings, terrorists will raise their poisonous heads and strike again, bringing a second wave of terror to an already unsettled society.

It is clear to even the casual observer that third world nations controlled by dictators will be able to obtain these weapons and begin their own nuclear programs in the near future. Nations could be held hostage by the possibilities this presents. We are already living in those perilous times.

2. THE INCREASE OF DEADLY PLAGUES AND VIRUSES

For nation will rise against nation, and kingdom against kingdom: and there will be famines, and pestilences, and earthquakes, in various places (Matthew 24:7).

When Jesus catalogued the signs of the end time, one sign was pestilence in various places. The Greek word is *loimos*, and it refers to "a plague or a disease." The Hebrew translation of this word can allude to a "plague that ends in death."

Several years ago, the sudden appearance of AIDS was a reminder to the world of this prophetic warning. Then Ebola suddenly appeared, striking poor African nations. This mysterious disease gradually melts the human organs and causes a horrible death. More recently, a flu-like virus called SARS struck China and spread through Asia, killing hundreds and infecting thousands.

Because people can travel from nation to nation in a matter of hours, invisible germs, viruses and diseases can also spread from nation to nation. Global travel makes this more possible now than at any other time in history. It also makes the danger more acute than at any other time in history.

The Centers for Disease Control in Atlanta informed the general public to begin expecting a steady wave of new infections, diseases and viruses to come to the shores of America.

The spread of a new virus could cause more than an epidemic—it could easily panic the planet, creating a pandemic. The appearance of strange plagues, diseases, and viruses is a fulfillment of the pestilences in various places that Christ warned about.

3. A Rise in Religious Fanatics

For false christs and false prophets will rise and show great signs and wonders to deceive, if possible, even the elect (Matthew 24:24).

Every religion has, from time to time, produced fanatics . . . some more than others. The Islamic religion has birthed a global terrorist network. In India, Hindu fanatics have burned missionaries and their families alive for the "crime" of preaching the gospel and feeding lepers.

Those who are members of the Ku Klux Klan (KKK) misquote and twist scriptures to support their own beliefs. Former Israeli Prime Minister Yitzak Rabin was assassinated by a young Jewish man who believed he was doing God a service by taking Rabin's life. He was trying to punish the former Prime Minister for giving away parts of Israel to the Palestinians.

Perhaps more human lives have been destroyed in the name of a religion than any other ideology. Each fanatic believes he is the defender of the true faith, and that others are deceived and deserve death. All fanatics believe they are operating in the will of God when they kill those who have an opposing belief.

Revelation 13 reveals a future religious leader arising shortly after the appearance of the Antichrist. Later identified as the False Prophet (16:13, 19:20, 20:10), this man will attempt to unite two global religions under his dominion. He will initiate the construction of a religious icon to the Antichrist, and will actually perform a supernatural miracle to make the icon speak and live (13:11-16). This religious fanatic will also initiate a universal system of buying and selling which will restrain those who do not accept his belief system from buying or selling (vv. 16-18).

In the beginning of human civilization, Cain killed his brother Abel because he was jealous over Abel's offering to God. The first murder involved religion. The final conflict at Jerusalem will involve a religious fanatic (the False Prophet) and his military commander, the Antichrist. The rise in fanatics, especially Islamic fanatics, is another evidence of the time of the end.

4. THE CRY OF INNOCENT BLOOD

And they cried with a loud voice, saying, "How long, O Lord, holy and true, until you judge and avenge our blood on those who dwell on the earth?" (Revelation 6:10).

Every year an average of 160,000 Christians die at the hands of religious fanatics, Islamic terrorists, and communist interrogators, or are murdered because they are Christians and will not deny their faith. As anti-Christian beliefs spread and the spirit of Antichrist rises around the globe, these numbers will increase throughout the world.

Christ predicted the city of Jerusalem would be destroyed and the Temple razed to the ground. He informed those in his generation that the judgment on the Holy City was because of previous generations shedding the blood of righteous saints and prophets who were sent to Israel (Matthew 23:30-36).

In the future, the religious system identified as mystery Babylon in Revelation 17 will come to an abrupt destruction because she shed the blood of prophets and saints (Revelation 17:6; 18:24). Just as Abel, the son of Adam, was slain and his blood cried out to God, the blood of millions of Christian martyrs throughout the centuries will cry out to God and demand retribution against those who willfully cut them off from the land of the living.

> And they cried with a loud voice, saying, "How long, O Lord, holy and true, dost thou not judge and avenge our blood on them that dwell on the earth?" (Revelation 6:10).

Not only has the blood of adults been slain, but millions of innocent babies have been cut off because of abortion. How long can the Lord allow the blood of the innocent to cry out and the cry for retribution not be heard in the ears of the Almighty?

Many of the judgments that will be unleashed during the great tribulation will be a result of the bloodshed that has swept the earth.

> For they have shed the blood of saints and prophets, and thou hast given them blood to drink; for they are worthy (Revelation 16:6).

The massive bloodshed on the earth will initiate the wrath of God upon the ungodly. Clearly, this is another reason why this generation must be a part of the last days.

5. THE SWIFT SPREAD OF THE GOSPEL MESSAGE

> And this gospel of the kingdom will be preached in all the world as a witness to all the nations, and then the end will come (Matthew 24:14).

From the time of Christ until the 1800's, men traveled the earth by ship, horseback, or on foot to preach the gospel. Journeying on the high seas could take several weeks or months, transferring from one port to another. Horses and carriages were used until the turn of the 20th century. My grandfather and my father have both told stories of walking from town to town to preach. The invention of the automobile enabled people to travel more frequently and between long distances. Eventually the modern jet airplane connected the continents within hours.

Not only has mass transportation brought the messengers of the gospel to the nations, but also mass communication has created the ability to bring the gospel message into homes across the world. Satellite, the Internet, television and short-wave radio can spread the gospel around the globe! More nations and individual souls are being reached at this present time than since the inception of the first-century church.

6. THE REVIVAL AMONG THE SONS AND DAUGHTERS

And it shall come to pass in the last days, says God, that I will pour out my Spirit on all flesh; your sons and your daughters shall prophesy. Your young men shall see visions, and your old men shall dream dreams. And on my menservants and on my maidservants I will pour out my Spirit in those days, and they shall prophesy (Acts 2:17, 18).

In North America, Europe, and the former communist block nations, there are many older denominations in which the congregation consists of a few faithful senior citizens who are loyal to the system. When these individuals pass away, the buildings will often be closed, or as in England, sold to Muslims to build a mosque.

The Lord has promised a revival among the sons and daughters. In nations such as Africa, Latin America, and Indonesia, there are huge mega-churches where as much as 80 percent of the congregation is under 30 years of age. Some churches are flooded with teenagers who are involved in missions, children's ministry and worship.

My dear friend Karen Wheaton began a youth ministry in Hamilton, Alabama, and today hundreds of youth are attending, directing the praise and worship, teaching, and being trained for the ministry. Each year there are youth conferences that draw thousands from across North America into large conference centers and stadiums!

This is all an indication that the prophecy of our sons and daughters encountering a fresh outpouring of the Spirit is beginning to happen!

7. The Rise of the Old Roman Empire

There are also seven kings. Five have fallen, one is, and the other has not yet come. And when he comes, he must continue a short time (Revelation 17:10).

For centuries, scholars have believed the nations in the old Roman Empire territory would reunite. This re-unification would have been impossible on the continent of Europe that once was divided between west and east, separated by communism and democracy. With the collapse of communist regimes in Eastern Europe and the change in the former Soviet Union, a united Europe became possible. However, this future united Europe will remain intact for a short space, until 10 nations are united under the umbrella of the kingdom of the beast.

Much has been said about the European Union (EU). This collection of European nations is growing into a powerful unit that will, in the future, become the strongest economic and political block in the world. Many scholars suggest that this rise in a new united Europe will eventually replace the strongman on the block, the United States of America.

8. THE NEW POPE AND THE SHAKING IN THE ROMAN CHURCH

And the woman that you saw is that great city, which reigns over the kings of the earth (Revelation 17:18).

Catholic hierarchy considers the scandal of homosexual and pedophile priests as one of the greatest challenges since the Protestant Reformation! There can be no comparison between the two. One is sexual perversion and the other was a spiritual revolution. One has led individuals into spiritual bondage, and the other has brought spiritual liberty.

To be sure, the Roman religious system has played, and will play, a premier role in the grand finale of prophetic events. Many Protestant scholars have interpreted the prophetic passages about the infamous scarlet harlot in Revelation 17, as the spiritual condition of the Roman church system (headquartered in Rome) in the final days.

With the death of Pope John Paul II, an interesting prophecy must be observed. In the 12th century, Malachy, an Irish-Catholic monk, penned a series of predictions involving the Roman Catholic Church. In his detailed predictions, he allegedly listed the number of popes who would sit on the throne of Rome until the Antichrist would arise and seek to destroy both the holy city and the Pope. According to Malachy, there would be a total of 112 popes from Malachy's time to the end.

Pope John Paul II is the 110th. According to Malachy's predictions, the 111th pope will be called the glory of the olive, and Malachy labeled the final pope as Peter the Roman. The pope following the 111th will be the one to fight the Antichrist of Bible prophecy.

If the prediction proves accurate, it would mean there are only two more popes from John Paul II until the conflict with the Antichrist.

Another belief being propagated among some of the many Roman Catholics who are now studying Biblical prophecy, is that the future false prophet identified in Revelation 13:11-16 will, in reality, be a pope who defects and denies the divinity of Christ. He will split the Roman church between those loyal to the church, and others who will turn against the Roman system.

Acting with the authority of 10 different kings or world leaders, this pope will destroy Rome, the city that has ruled over nations and influenced kings of the earth (Revelation 17:18).

If we conclude that the Antichrist is from an Islamic background, and the False Prophet is directly linked to the Roman church, then the Roman religious system will see some major disruptions and conflicts in the future. Those who are loyal to the system are instructed in Revelation 18:4: "Come out of her, my people, lest you share in her sins, and lest you receive of her plagues."

Former Muslims have told me that the major rift between Islam and historic Christianity is the Christian belief that Jesus is the Son of God. No Muslim accepts this view. In fact, Islamic teaching denies any possibility that God could, or ever would, produce a son. If a future Pontiff of Rome would teach that Jesus was a prophet but not the Son of God, then he would be hailed and accepted by most Muslims.

According to the New Testament, to deny that Christ is the Son of God and to reject the relationship between the Father and the Son is the spirit of Antichrist (1 John 2:18,

2:22, 4:3; 2 John 7). The changes in the Roman church will play a part in the final days.

9. THE BATTLE OVER JERUSALEM

Behold, I will make Jerusalem a cup of drunkenness to all the surrounding peoples, when they lay siege against Judah and Jerusalem. And it shall happen in that day that I will make Jerusalem a very heavy stone for all peoples; all who would heave it away will surely be cut in pieces, though all nations of the earth are gathered against it (Zechariah 12:2, 3).

How could one city in the Middle East be the controversy among nations? Secular individuals will never understand the constant news coverage, the carnage left by homicide bombers, and the anti-Israeli protests in the territories, until they understand the clash is an ancient feud and a religious struggle between two relatives.

The struggle began when Abraham fathered a son, Ishmael, through an Egyptian wife. Later, Abraham's covenant wife, Sarah, conceived a son promised from God 25 years before Isaac's birth. At age 13, Ishmael and his mother, Hagar, were forced out of the house and the young boy became an archer, dwelling in the wilderness.

The conflict intensified with Isaac's twin sons, Jacob and Esau. Jacob, the younger, conceived a plot to steal the blessing of Esau. The strategy worked, and another family rift continued for 20 years. It should be noted that the sons of Isaac and Ishmael both buried their father, Abraham; and Jacob and Esau made restoration with each other (Genesis 33:1-16). The real rift began when a man named Shechem, son of Hamor, raped Dinah, the daughter of Jacob. Dinah's two brothers, Simeon and Levi, retaliated by killing all the men in the family. Thus began a conflict with the tribes from the Promised Land.

10. The Palestinian State

Do not rejoice, all you of Philistia, because the rod that struck you is broken; for out of the serpent's roots will come forth a viper, and its offspring will be a fiery flying serpent (Isaiah 14:29).

The Palestinian people desire an independent state. Those living in the land prior to 1948 believe the Jews possess the land illegally. Most Muslims believe Israel is a modern nation established by the West. They deny the Jews ever had a nation, and they deny there was ever a Jewish Temple on the Temple Mount platform. In reality, the true Palestinian state should be located in the modern nation of Jordan, and not Israel.

When we consider that Isaac's son, Esau, is identified as Edom, and the Edomites are linked to those people who have lived in Israel for hundreds of centuries, then the remedy is clear. The country of Jordan is actually the true Palestinian state. If the Palestinian people want self-rule, a government, and financial stability, they should secure a large portion of Jordan and build their state in that region.

This is never going to happen, because the rich Persian Gulf states use the Palestinians like a pawn on a chess board in order to put Israel in check, hoping one day to declare checkmate and leave Israel with no possible way out.

The plan is clear: the Palestinian Authority, under Yassir Arafat, was given millions of dollars to help the Palestinian people. Instead, the senseless leader bought personal property for himself and his cronies in Europe. With money for the Palestinian people, he purchased new Mercedes-Benz automobiles for his family members.

Instead of bringing hope and jobs, and rebuilding the refugee camps into clean livable communities, he has chosen to keep the cash and keep the Palestinians in poverty. The strategy is that if the Palestinian people sense hopelessness, poverty and gloom, Israel will always be blamed.

This mentality of gloom is also a hot breeding ground for recruiting new suicide bombers. People who have freedom, education and jobs are less likely to follow some half-wit imam who is twisting the Koran for his own benefit. The Palestinian conflict must come to a head. The combination of these ten factors leads me to believe we are in the time of the end.

PRESENT DAY HISTORY

Prior to Israel's rebirth in 1948, the nation called Palestine consisted of Arabs, Christians and Jews. The rebirth of Israel caused an immediate outrage among the surrounding Arab nations, mostly because Palestine was considered an Islamic state. For Jews to possess Palestine was nothing short of blasphemy in the eyes of loyal Muslims.

From 1948 to now, Muslims have continually sought to remove the Jews from inside Israel. Some have twisted their religious beliefs to persuade young men to be soldiers to liberate Palestine by killing as many Jews as possible within their own borders.

Jerusalem is the root of this conflict. The two Islamic mosques on the Temple Mount platform in Jerusalem are the source of the bitterness. Jerusalem is Islam's third holiest city and the Dome of the Rock is the third holiest mosque. As long as Jerusalem remains the legal and spiritual capital of the Jewish state, there will always be terror cells secretly planning deadly assaults against innocent Jewish families attempting to live peacefully in Israel. The debate over the status of Jerusalem is becoming more heated and the waters of conflict are brewing. Terrorism is spreading from border to border.

These 10 stepping stones are early indications of future prophetic fulfillments. The current acceleration of events will climax within one generation—perhaps ours!

CHAPTER 9

THIS GENERATION SHALL NOT PASS

The meaning of a generation

Assuredly, I say to you, this gener-

ation will by no means pass away till

all these things take place. Heaven

and earth will pass away, but My

words will by no means pass away

(Matthew 24:34, 35).

As a teenage minister just called to preach, I remember piling stacks of books, news articles, and study guides on my desk and spending countless hours poring over the information, scribbling notes, and completing messages with an old typewriter that could have been an antique from World War II. I was amazed at how many times other ministers had projected dates and times for the Lord's return.

Most calculations began in 1948 when Israel was reestablished as a nation, and projected forward to mark the final generation. Some suggested the coming of the Lord for the church would be in 1981, and added seven years for the Tribulation, climaxing the "end of the age" in 1988. Others focused on 1988 and predicted the Tribulation would be after the coming of Christ.

Most prophetic teachers were determined to make a generation a 40-year time period. I began my research by asking, "What is the Biblical meaning of the word *generation?*" I discovered the word could allude to an age, a generation, a time or a nation. I also discovered that when the Bible uses the word *generation,* there were different time periods connected to the word, depending on what the Scripture is alluding to.

THE GENERATIONS OF HEAVEN AND EARTH

This is the history (generations) of the heavens and the earth when they were created, in the day that the Lord God made the earth and the heavens (Genesis 2:4).

The six days of creation are comparable to six 1,000-year periods of human government. The generations of heaven and earth can be considered one thousand year cycles, since "with the Lord one day is as a thousand years, and a thousand years as one day"(2 Peter 3:8). Before the flood, men lived to be extremely old by present standards. Adam died at 930 years of age, just 70 years short of 1,000 years (Genesis 5:5). Methuselah lived 969 years, 31 years short of a complete millennium!

THE GENERATION OF ABRAHAM'S DESCENDANTS

Then He said to Abram: "Know certainly that your descendants will be strangers in a land that is not theirs, and will serve them, and they will afflict them four hundred years. And also the nation whom they serve I will judge; afterward they shall come out with great possessions. Now as for you, you shall go to your fathers in peace; you shall be buried at a good old age. But in the fourth generation they shall return here, for the iniquity of the Amorites is not yet complete" (Genesis 15:13-16).

This prediction from the Almighty alluded to the time when Israel would be in Egypt for 400 years. After becoming slaves to Pharaoh, the Hebrews cried to God for deliverance, and God remembered His covenant with Abraham (Exodus 2:24).

Moses brought the nation out of Egyptian captivity, across the Red Sea, and to the Promised Land. God said this event would occur in 400 years, or in the fourth generation. In this case, if the fourth generation is after 400 years, then the average of one generation is 100 years. The generations in Abraham's time were longer than at the present time, because men lived longer. Abraham lived to be 175 years old (Genesis 25:7), Isaac died at age 180 (35:28), Jacob died at age 147 (47:28), and Joseph died at age 110 (50:26). In this example a generation was a period of 100 years.

The Generation of Unbelief

For forty years I was grieved with that generation, and said, "It is a people who go astray in their hearts, and they do not know My ways." So I swore in My wrath, "They shall not enter My rest" (Psalms 95:10, 11).

All Hebrews 20 years of age and up who followed Moses out of Egypt died in the wilderness, except two men—Joshua and Caleb (Numbers 14:29-30). The wilderness experience was known as a "generation of unbelief." The Apostle Paul wrote much about their failure to believe God's promises (Hebrews 3:8-19).

After this event, the number 40 was always understood in the Bible to be a number for testing, trials and a generation of unbelief. This was illustrated when God gave Ninevah 40 days to repent (Jonah 3:3-5). Elijah was tried for 40 days (1 Kings 19:7-9).

This concept was further illustrated during the time of Christ. In approximately A.D. 30, Jesus rebuked His generation for their unbelief. He predicted in vivid language what would come upon His generation for their unbelief and for their shedding the blood of the prophets.

That upon you may come all the righteous blood shed upon the earth, from the blood of righteous Abel unto the blood of Zacharias son of Barachias, whom ye slew between the temple and the altar. Verily I say unto you, all these things shall come upon this generation (Matthew 23:35, 36 KJV).

About 40 years later Jesus' words came to pass. The Holy City was surrounded and destroyed, along with the sacred Temple. During that period, there was no repentance among the people. They were truly a generation of unbelief, similar to the generation of unbelief in the wilderness. Thus a generation was 40 years.

4. THE GENERATION OF A MAN

After this Job lived one hundred and forty years, and saw his children and grandchildren for four generations. So Job died, old and full of days (Job 42:16, 17).

Job lived 140 years, or four generations. If we divide the number four into 140, the average of a generation is 35 years. This number seems to be the average number of a generation when we examine the average age of when a man's first son was born after the flood.

Reference	Person	First Son Born
◆ Genesis 11:10	Shem	at age 100
◆ v. 12	Arphaxad	at age 35
◆ v. 14	Salah	at age 30
◆ v. 16	Eber	at age 34
◆ v. 18	Peleg	at age 30
◆ v. 20	Reu	at age 32
◆ v. 22	Serug	at age 30
◆ v. 24	Nahor	at age 29
◆ v. 26	Terah	at age 70
◆ v. 21:5	Abraham	at age 100

HOW LONG IS A GENERATION?

The average age of a man when his first son was born was 49 years. If we omit Shem and Abraham, then the average age was 36. You can see that the length of a generation is actually determined by what period in history you are referring to, and the concept of time before and after the flood of Noah.

Prior to the flood, men lived longer, married later, and had children much later in life. Following the flood, the average lifespan was reduced, along with the average

age when the first child was born. After the revelation of the Torah to Moses, man's days were reduced to an average of 70 (Psalms 90:10).

Much has been made of the statement "this generation." The preterist theory teaches that all of the signs of Matthew 24 have already been fulfilled. Those who advocate that belief teach that all things were fulfilled prior to, and at the time of, the destruction of the Temple in A.D. 70. They believe this because Jesus said that this generation shall not pass until all is fulfilled. He was addressing His disciples, so they believe all of Matthew 24 has been fulfilled.

Certain predictions from Matthew 24 did come to pass in the destruction of the Temple, but certainly not all. For example:

The Prediction	When Fulfilled
Jerusalem surrounded by armies	*In A.D. 66 and 70*
The Temple building will be destroyed	*Ultimately. in A.D. 70*
Not one stone left upon another	*In 70 A.D.*
Christians fleeing for safety	*Christians fled to Jordan*
False prophets and false christs	*Until the destruction*

Other signs listed in Matthew 24 never transpired before or in A.D. 70. For example:

♦ There was never a darkening of the sun and moon or a shaking of the powers of heaven (Matthew 24:29) during the destruction of the

Temple, but there will be during the future Tribulation (Revelation 6:12).

♦ The sign of the Son of Man in heaven never appeared in or around A.D. 70 (Matthew 24:30).

♦ The Son of Man never appeared in the clouds of glory in or around A.D. 70 (Mathew 24:30), but He will appear at the end of the future Tribulation (Revelation 1:7).

♦ The tribes of the earth did not mourn because of Christ's return in A.D. 70 (Matthew 24:30), but they will all see Him coming at His return to earth (Revelation 1:7).

One interpretation of Christ's statement, "this generation shall not pass," is that He was revealing parallel signs that would happen during two different time periods. One generation was the generation in the first century that witnessed the signs of the destruction of Jerusalem and the Holy Temple. Another group would be a generation that would see similar signs in their time, and would not pass until they experienced the Lord's return to earth.

ANOTHER INTERPRETATION

When Christ said "this generation" to His disciples, He meant the generation who sees the signs fulfilled would not pass. A hundred years ago, if a minister had told a group of Iraqis that a dictator was coming whose statue would one day be torn to the ground, the Iraqis might have asked, "When will it happen?"

The minister might have said, "You will see an army surround Baghdad. It will be at a time when great distress and rumors of war are happening. This generation will not pass until all these things are accomplished." A casual reader may think that the people standing there at that time would be alive when it happens. In reality, the minister is saying, "The generation who sees the army surrounding Baghdad will be present to see the fall of the dictator and the statue."

THERE IS A GENERATION

Just as a generation witnessed the Messiah's first appearance as Isaiah's suffering servant, there will be an end-time generation who will see the Lamb of God become the Lion of the Tribe of Judah and return as the conquering King. I believe the unique signs that transpired before the first appearance of Christ will be repeated before the return of our Lord.

First Century Signs	Signs of His Return
♦ Murder of innocent babies (Matthew 2:16)	Murder of innocent babies
♦ A global government (Rome)	A global government is forming
♦ Taxation was heavy (Luke 2:1)	Taxation is heavy
♦ Strange cosmic signs (Matthew 2:2)	Much cosmic activity
♦ Warnings in dreams (Matthew 2:13)	Dreams will be given (Acts 2:17)
♦ Major roads were built	Major transportation available
♦ One main language (Greek)	One main language (English)
♦ Messianic expectations were high	Messianic expectations are high

One generation experienced a series of signs and prophetic fulfillments that indicated the Messiah had come. Another end-time generation will experience signs that will indicate the Messiah is soon to return to set up His visible kingdom.

Based on the fulfillment of the signs, the ancient prophecies and the amazing parallels, I believe we are the generation who will experience the return of the Messiah. It also means that this unbelieving generation will be the one that will eventually be thrust into the final Great Tribulation of prophecy.

WHY IT HAS NOT HAPPENED YET

If we are the generation who will see and experience many signs of the end of the age and prophetic fulfillments, many people wonder what is delaying the start of the seven-year Tribulation and the revealing of the future Antichrist of Bible prophecy. There are four main reasons.

THE FULLNESS OF INIQUITY

When God confirmed His covenant with Abraham, He revealed that Abraham's descendants would be taken to a strange nation for 400 years. Afterwards, God would bring them out to judge the inhabitants of the Promised Land, including a huge nation called the Amorites. The reason for the 400-year delay was that the iniquity of the Amorites was not yet full (Genesis 15:16). Over a period of years, the sins and iniquities of a nation increase. As the cup of iniquity becomes full, God will begin to release His judgments on earth.

Daniel 8:23 indicates the future Antichrist will rise on the global scene when the "transgressors are come to full." According to the Book of Revelation, there is a cup in heaven that must become full before God unleashes His final judgments. It is called the cup "of the wine of the fierceness of God's wrath" (Revelation 16:19).

It is interesting that there are seven vials in heaven that will one day be poured out on the earth in the form of severe cosmic and ecological judgments. There are seven continents on earth and seven vials filled with the wrath of God. Could each vial represent one of the seven continents where God's judgment will strike the earth? The full thrust of God's judgments on the earth will not be felt until the iniquity of mankind is full and the cup of God's winepress is full!

The Age of Grace

The second reason we are not experiencing global wrath from the Almighty is because we are presently in the dispensation of the grace of God (Ephesians 3:2). Some scholars also identify this as the *church age*. Because God is presently dealing with humanity in the form of mercy and grace, there will be times of selective, but not universal, judgment.

In 1 Corinthians 9:17, Paul mentioned the "dispensation of the gospel." The Greek word *dispensation* means "the administration of a house." The purpose of the church is to administer the grace of God to this generation, until the assignment of the church to preach the gospel around the world is complete.

When the church completes its assignment, the end will come (Matthew 24:14). It will mark the end of one dispensation and the beginning of another. Between the conclusion of the church age and the beginning of the Messiah's thousand-year reign, there will be a clash between two kingdoms (Satan's and God's), and a seven-year Tribulation. The Tribulation is being restrained because of the church's mission to reach the nations with the message of eternal life through Jesus Christ.

We're Still Here

We are still on earth. One main thread woven throughout the Scripture is that God does not judge the righteous and unrighteous on the same level. He does not allow the righteous to suffer His wrath along with the unrighteous. As previously stated, God always provides a fair warning and a way of escape to those who serve Him.

The fact that the body of Christ is still ministering on earth is an indication that we are a part of restraining the wrath from being released. Another example can be found in the story of Lot. When Lot was warned to flee Sodom and Gomorrah, the angels instructed him to immediately escape to a local mountain (Genesis 19:17). In fear, Lot instead requested to escape to a small city named Zoar (v. 22).

Zoar is listed as one of the five main cities in the area of Sodom and Gomorrah. Genesis 14:1-3 lists these five cities as Sodom, Gomorrah, Admah, Zeboim and Zoar. When the fire and brimstone rained upon Sodom, it destroyed four of these five cities that were located in the Valley of Siddim (v. 3). Zoar was the only city of the five that was not destroyed.

> And he said to him, "See, I have favored you concerning this thing also, in that I will not overthrow this city for which you

have spoken. Hurry, escape there. For I cannot do anything until you arrive there" (19:21, 22).

Three important points must be made concerning this statement by the angel of the Lord: First, the angels of God could not initiate the destruction of the cities until Lot, his wife and two daughters were physically removed from the city. Second, the city of Zoar was actually included on the hit list for God's judgment, but was spared because Lot made Zoar his new home. Third, only after Lot was safe in Zoar did the fiery destruction consume Sodom and Gomorrah (vv. 23, 24).

The spiritual principle of protection for the righteous is clear in the flood account and the deliverance of Lot from Sodom. Three truths are also parallel when we explore the fact that the Lord will not send the Tribulation on earth until the church is safe with Him in heaven.

Just as the angels were restrained from destroying Sodom until Lot was removed from the city, so the wrath of God cannot be released until believers are physically removed from the earth through the catching away, the Rapture. Believers are not appointed to wrath (1 Thessalonians 5:9), and are told to pray to be accounted worthy to escape the coming Tribulation (Luke 21:36).

One reason judgment has not yet come is because multitudes of born again believers are living in cities around the world. Because Lot chose Zoar, God spared this small city from destruction. The presence of true Christians in the major cities actually restrains the fullness of God's wrath from being released in those cities.

Only after Lot went up the mountain and reached the city (Zoar) did the four cities of the plain face sudden annihilation. Only after the church has been removed to the mountain of God in heaven will the sealed book containing the first stages of God's judgments on earth be opened (Revelation 5, 6).

After 400 years of living in Egypt, one generation of Hebrews experienced the Exodus. After 100 years of preparing the ark, one generation in Noah's time experienced a deluge, the flood of Noah. After a one-day warning, one generation of people was burned into destruction by the fire of God's wrath on the cities of the plain.

After 1,500 years of expectations, one generation was blessed to see the birth, ministry, death and resurrection of the Messiah. A generation of 40 years followed Christ's ascension, and that unbelieving generation lived to see the destruction of Jerusalem and the Holy Temple.

There is a generation that will live to hear the trumpet of God sound and see the Lord coming in the air! If we are that generation, then we must watch and pray if we are to be accounted worthy to escape the coming Tribulation and to stand before the Son of God (Luke 21:36).

After years of research, I agree with many prophetic teachers that we are the first generation to witness such a culmination of numerous prophetic signs and indicators occurring at the same time. The apostle Paul wrote that we (believers) are not in darkness that the day should overtake us unaware (1 Thessalonians 5:4).

There is a generation who will be watching, praying and waiting. We are that generation!

CHAPTER 10

UNUSUAL AND DIFFICULT SCRIPTURES

Explaining prophetic passages from historic and Hebraic perspectives

Nevertheless we, according to His promise, look for new heavens and a new earth in which righteousness dwells. Therefore, beloved, looking forward to these things, be diligent to be found by Him in peace, without spot and blameless; and consider that the longsuffering of our Lord is salvation—as also our beloved brother Paul, according to the wisdom given to him, has written to you, as also in all his epistles, speaking in them of these things, in which are some things hard to understand, which untaught and unstable people twist to their own destruction, as they do also the rest of the Scriptures (2 Peter 3:13-16).

*I*n the first century church, two prominent leaders, Paul and Peter, had some differences of opinion. Paul was the minister to the Gentile branch of the church, and Peter remained loyal to the Jewish branch of the church. God directed Peter to preach to the first Gentiles in Acts 10.

Later, Peter began teaching that Gentile believers should be circumcised as a sign of their conversion to Christ. Paul said he "withstood Peter to his face." He accused Peter of being two-faced and acting one way when he was with Jewish believers and another way when fellowshiping with Gentiles:

> Now when Peter had come to Antioch, I withstood him to his face, because he was to be blamed; for before certain men came from James, he would eat with the Gentiles; but when they came, he withdrew and separated himself, fearing those who were of the circumcision. And the rest of the Jews also played the hypocrite with him, so that even Barnabas was carried away with their hypocrisy (Galatians 2:11-13).

Toward the conclusion of Peter's ministry, he made it clear that Paul preached certain things difficult to understand. Paul had received numerous revelations from God when he spent lengthy time in prayer in the desert of Arabia (Galatians 1:17, 18). These revelations were penned in Paul's epistles, and no other apostle had received this illumination from God. If Peter said some things were difficult to understand, then we must make a great effort today to expound and explain certain scriptures.

There are often passages of scripture that are difficult to fully understand from a western perspective. This is because the Bible was written during a 2,500 year time period and from an eastern concept of society and ancient history. To better understand the many unusual passages in the Bible, one must research the historical setting, the original meaning of the words, and the context in which they were written. This type of research often unveils a richer meaning that the reader can better appreciate.

THE PARABLE OF THE FIG TREE

Now learn this parable from the fig tree: When its branch has already become tender and puts forth leaves, you know that summer is near. So you also, when you see all these things, know that it is near—at the doors (Matthew 24:32, 33).

In Matthew 24, the disciples asked Christ for the sign of His coming and the end of the age (Matthew 24:3). After a lengthy discourse describing wars, famines, pestilence, deception and various cosmic signs, Christ concluded with the Parable of the Fig Tree.

Normally, when Christ spoke in a parable, it was a story with a hidden meaning that He often revealed privately to His disciples. In this case, He simply said, "Learn the parable of the fig tree." Then He stated a known fact: when you see the fig leaves, you know summer is near. It appeared to me that this parable was not totally complete, or perhaps the disciples were already aware of a fig tree parable, and needed no further explanation.

During one of my journeys to Israel in the early 1990s I asked our tour guide, Gideon Shor, if there was a parable of the fig tree in the Bible. He said there was, and suggested I turn to the story of the fig tree in Judges 9:10-13. After reading the passage, I knew this passage contained no prophetic insight relating to Christ's return. Looking puzzled, Gideon asked, "What parable are you talking about?" I replied, "The one Jesus spoke about in Matthew 24:32. He grinned and said, "Oh, you must mean the parable in the Song of Solomon!" We turned to the Song of Solomon and read the following scripture:

> The voice of my beloved! Behold, he comes leaping upon the mountains, skipping upon the hills. My beloved is like a gazelle or a young stag. Behold, he stands behind our wall; he is looking through the windows, gazing through the lattice.
>
> My beloved spoke, and said to me: "Rise up, my love, my fair one, and come away. For lo, the winter is past, the rain is over and gone. The flowers appear on the earth; the time of singing has come, and the voice of the turtledove is heard in our land. The fig tree puts forth her green figs, and the vines with the tender grapes give a good smell. Rise up, my love, my fair one, and come away!" (Song of Solomon 2:8-13).

After musing over these verses, I began to see the picture of the parable of the fig tree that Christ's disciples were already aware of! The Song of Solomon is a book about a bride and a bridegroom. In this passage, the bride (the church) is waiting for her bridegroom to appear. He has been observing her from the secret place from behind a wall in the upper lattice (heaven).

Suddenly, she hears his voice. The Lord will descend in a shout and those in the grave will hear His voice. After the voice, he is seen leaping on the mountains and skipping on the hills. When Christ returns for the church, His feet will not touch the ground, but He will be in the air, above the hills and mountains; and He will skip from mountain to mountain to gather the dead in Christ and the living to Himself!

In verses 10 and 13, the bridegroom states twice, "Arise my love." Why two times? I believe this is a reference to the resurrection and the catching away of those who know Christ! In the New Testament, the dead will be called to rise first, and then we who are alive will be transformed and called to rise and meet Him in the air. The bridegroom says twice, "Come away!" John saw a preview of this event when he was told by the voice from heaven to "come up hither" (Revelation 4:1, 2).

The voice of the Bridegroom, His call to His bride, and His command to arise and come away happen when the "fig tree puts forth her green leaves." This alludes to the late Spring months, just before Summer.

KEEP YOUR EYES OPEN

Many times Christ would pray with His eyes wide open. He would demand that His disciples should "watch as well as pray" (Luke 21:36). Christ gave three main reasons for watching:

1. Watch because you don't know when I will return (Matthew 24:42).
2. Watch so that you do not enter into temptation (Matthew 26:41).
3. Watch and pray to be counted worthy to escape the Tribulation (Luke 21:36).

In Christ's time, the word *watch* alluded to the watchmen who were positioned on the walls surrounding the Temple compound in Jerusalem. Special priests were assigned to open the massive gates in the morning and lock them at night. Throughout the night, Temple guards (watchmen) would use torches to observe the surrounding area to see if an invading army or enemy was lurking in the distance or hiding beneath the walls.

The greatest challenge for a watchman, or Temple guard, was to not be caught sleeping. Occasionally a Temple officer, called "the ruler of the mountain of the house," would randomly walk around the Temple and inspect the guards to see if they were awake and at their posts, or if they were sleeping. If he caught them napping, he would strike them with a large stick.

It was also permissible to strip the sleeping guard and burn his clothes. According to the Talmud, R. Eliezar Ben Jacob said, "They once found my mother's son asleep and they burned his clothes." This may be what Christ alluded to in Revelation 16:15 when he warned, "Behold, I am coming as a thief. Blessed is he who watches, and keeps his garments, lest he walk naked and they see his shame."

Those who become spiritually sluggish and unconcerned will be caught unaware at the sudden return of Christ; and will be exposed for their unspiritual, lukewarm condition.

THE SECOND AND THIRD WATCH

Blessed are those servants whom the master, when he comes, will find watching. Assuredly, I say to you that he will gird himself and have them sit down to eat, and will come and serve them. And if he should come in the second watch, or come in the third watch, and find them so, blessed are those servants (Luke 12:37, 38).

Another interesting scripture related to the watch is in Luke 12. Jesus warned His followers to stay alert (awake) because He would return suddenly and at a time they may not expect. He mentioned the second and third watches. The Jews divided the day in the same manner God did at the time of Creation. "The evening and morning were the first day" (Genesis 1:5). The Jewish day ends at sunset and a new day begins at sunrise. The time frame was 12 hours plus 12 hours, which totals 24 hours of one complete day.

Later, during the Roman occupation, the Jews adapted the Roman reckoning of a day into four watches.

+ The first watch was from sunset until nine at night.

+ The second watch was from nine at night until midnight.

+ The third watch was from midnight until three in the morning.

+ The fourth watch was from three in the morning until sunrise.

In the English translation of the Bible, these watches are alluded to in Mark 13:35. The first watch is "even," the second is "midnight," the third watch is called "cockcrowing," and the fourth watch is called "morning."

Jesus often awoke long before daylight to pray (Mark 1:35). On one occasion, He was praying at the fourth watch (Matthew 14:25). The fourth watch began at three o'clock in the morning and concluded at six in the morning, near the time of sunrise. This was the time many fishermen were casting their nets at the Sea of Galilee. It was also a favorite prayer time for Jesus.

The second watch was from nine o'clock at night until midnight, and the third watch was from midnight until three in the morning.

The final watch, from three to six in the morning, was the most difficult time for a Temple watchman to stay awake. This was the common time for the Temple officers to make their unexpected rounds to see if the guards were asleep. Jesus knew that if we sleep, the enemy could successfully sow tares among the wheat and disrupt the harvest (Matthew 13:25).

KEEPING YOUR LAMPS TRIMMED AND BURNING

Let your waist be girded and your lamps burning (Luke 12:35).

Most people are familiar with candles, but few are aware of the oil lamps that were used in the Roman time. There were two major types of lamps: one was a common oil lamp used in the home and the other, used at night, was an oil lamp connected to a large pole that looked like a large torch.

The oil lamps were formed out of clay. Various designs were imprinted on the clay while it was wet, and the clay later hardened. There was a small hole in the center to pour in the olive oil, and a small opening on one end to place a wick. The oil lamps were placed on windowsills or on a stone that protruded out of the wall of the house. Every room often had a place for an oil lamp. The oil in the lamp had to be renewed from time to time, and the wick had to be changed often.

When a wick was not trimmed or replaced, it would burn and eventually produce a black smoke that would fill the atmosphere of the house. Keeping the lamp trimmed and burning involved keeping fresh oil in the lamp. Keeping it trimmed alludes to trimming the wick to prevent black smoke from filling the atmosphere. From a practical perspective, oil can allude to the Holy Spirit and the anointing. We are to be continually filled with the Holy Spirit (Ephesians 5:18).

In the Parable of the Ten Virgins, the call came at midnight that the bridegroom was coming (Matthew 25:6). At that moment, the 10 virgins awoke, only to discover that five of them were short of the oil needed for their lamps. The oil lamps in this story would have been the types that were placed on top of a wooden pole. It was common to keep a pouch of extra oil in case it was needed. The message here is that we should always be prepared, stay awake, and stay filled with the Holy Spirit!

As Fast as Lightning

For as the lightning cometh out of the east, and shineth even unto the west; so shall also the coming of the Son of man be (Matthew 24:27, KJV).

The speed and swiftness of Christ's return is compared to lightning, which sweeps from east to west in a moment's time. The speed of light is slightly over 186,000 miles per second. The earth is 25,000 miles in circumference. This means that if lightning struck in one spot and traveled around the earth, it could sweep around the globe seven and one-half times per second. The return of Christ will be so swift it will be as fast as lightning rushing from the east to the west.

When Paul wrote about the return of Christ, he indicated that those living at the time would be "changed in a moment in the twinkling of an eye" (1 Corinthians 15:52). The phrase "in a moment" indicates the quickness of the activity.

The Greek word for moment is *atomos,* from the word *tomoteros.* The word alludes to a single, swift action. The phrase "twinkling of an eye" also indicates the sudden physical change that will strike a believer at the very second Christ returns. There will be no time to pray, repent or intercede.

Years ago, a minister stated that a major computer company tested how long it takes to blink an eye. He indicated it was a single hundredth of a second. This is why Christ continually demanded that His loyal disciples should consistently watch and pray, so that they would not be caught unaware at His return.

Some people believe if they are unprepared for Christ's return, then they will have time to repent of their sins moments before the living believers are changed and caught up to meet the Lord in the air. They assume that the "shout, voice of the archangel, and the trump of God" mentioned in 1 Thessalonians 4:16 will take some time to occur and during this brief moment, they can repent and make it by the "skin of their teeth." I believe only those who are looking for the return of the Lord will actually hear the shout, the voice and the trumpet of God.

An example is when God spoke audibly to Christ in John 12:28-30. Christ asked God to glorify His name. God spoke from heaven in an audible voice. Those who were standing by reacted in different ways. Some said the voice was only thunder, others said it was the voice of an angel, and others recognized it was the voice of God.

Not everyone heard God's voice, just as not everyone will hear God's voice at the Rapture. The reaction to what you will hear is related to whom you are listening to! On seven occasions during the messages to the seven churches, Christ said, "He who has an ear, let him hear what the Spirit says to the churches."

ONE TAKEN AND THE OTHER LEFT

Then two men will be in the field: one will be taken and the other left. Two women will be grinding at the mill: one will be taken and the other left. Watch therefore, for you do not know what hour your Lord is coming (Matthew 24:40-42).

Many prophecy scholars believe this verse alludes to the time Christ will return to earth at the conclusion of the Tribulation to introduce his 1,000-year reign (Revelation 20:4). The concept is taught that those in the parable who are taken are removed from earth because they have received the Mark of the Beast, and those who remain are those who refused the Mark. If this is true, then those removed are taken to hell, along with the beast and false prophet (Revelation 19:20). Those who remain will rule with Christ.

The difficulty with this interpretation is the other verses linked to this passage, as well as good common sense. Jesus was emphasizing the importance of watching for His return (Matthew 24:42). After one is taken from the field and another is taken from the grinding mill, Christ said:

> But know this, that if the master of the house had known what hour the thief would come, he would have watched and not allowed his house to be broken into. Therefore you also be ready, for the Son of Man is coming at an hour you do not expect (Matthew 24:43, 44).

In Greek, the word *goodman* means "the head of the house." The owner of the house was to watch to prevent his house from being broken into. In the parable, the sudden return of the Lord had broken up his house so that some people were missing and the head of the house remained. The goodman was filled with regret and sorrow, since part of the family was missing.

The proof that this parable speaks of the Rapture can also be seen where Christ compared the breakup of the house to a thief coming in unexpectedly. The theme of Christ coming as a thief is found in many scriptures in the New Testament:

> But you, brethren, are not in darkness, so that this day should overtake you as a thief (1 Thessalonians 5:4).

For you yourselves know perfectly that the day of the Lord so comes as a thief in the night (1 Thessalonians 5:2).

But the day of the Lord will come as a thief in the night (2 Peter 3:10).

I will come upon you as a thief, and you will not know what hour I will come upon you (Revelation 3:3).

A thief comes unannounced and unexpectedly, and usually targets something of value in a home. He enters the house, steals the goods, and then departs without anyone's knowledge. The coming of Christ will be in the same fashion. The valuable goods will be the precious souls who have been purchased by the blood of Christ and will be taken before the time of God's wrath, or raptured and taken into heaven.

Second Coming Time Zones

I tell you, in that night there will be two men in one bed: the one will be taken and the other will be left. Two women will be grinding together: the one will be taken and the other left. Two men will be in the field: the one will be taken and the other left (Luke 17:34-36).

Two thousand years ago, civilizations flourished in and around the Mediterranean Sea area. Three major empires had dominated this region: The Egyptian, Babylonian and Grecian Empires. In Christ's day, the Roman Empire occupied the nations surrounding the Mediterranean Sea and made inroads into the areas of Asia, Northern Africa, Great Britain and Spain. This was the known world of that time and the common trade routes for ships and merchants. Two thousand years ago, no one was aware of the land that would later be named South America, the United States, or Canada.

To be more specific, people living in the Roman Empire were unaware of the existence of various time zones on the other side of the world. When it is five o'clock on the east coast of America, it is midnight in Israel, since Israel is seven hours ahead. In Christ's day, men and women worked during the day and slept at night. At that time, there was no work activity that demanded a nightshift job. Most people were farmers and shepherds, and went to bed at sunset and arose at sunrise.

Jesus made an interesting statement when he said that at His return, "Two would be in the bed, one taken and the other left, and two would be working in the field, one taken and the other left." We now understand that, at His coming, part of the world will be working and part of the world will be sleeping! Jesus actually revealed there would be different time zones on earth at His coming, something that was not realized 2,000 years ago before the unknown continents became populated with cities and nations.

For example, if Christ returns at midnight in Israel's time, it will be five in the afternoon on the east coast of America, two in the afternoon in California, and so forth. Some will be caught up to meet the Lord from the workplace and others will be snatched out of their beds where they are sleeping.

THE FRIEND OF THE BRIDEGROOM

He who has the bride is the bridegroom; but the friend of the bridegroom, who stands and hears him, rejoices greatly because of the bridegroom's voice (John 3:29).

In the ancient Jewish wedding, there were two witnesses involved in the wedding. One was a witness for the bride and one was for the groom. During the great Tribulation, God will send two witnesses to Jerusalem to evangelize a remnant of Jewish believers (Revelation 11:1-6). Many scholars identify these two witnesses as the two prophets who have never physically died, but were caught up into heaven—Enoch and Elijah.

The prophet Enoch was a Gentile, since he lived before Abraham. Elijah, however, is one of the chief Jewish prophets. The Christian church consists of both Gentiles and Jews; therefore, one of the two witnesses during the future Tribulation will represent the Gentile branch and the other, Elijah, will represent the Jewish branch.

In Christ's time, the friend of the bridegroom was a man selected by the bridegroom to conduct all the details of the marriage agreement on his behalf. Once a Jewish man was espoused to a woman, he was unable to see her or personally speak to her for about 11 months. The friend of the bridegroom carried personal messages between the bride and the bridegroom during the period they were apart.

The bridegroom's friend assisted with all personal matters until the time the couple was united under the *chupah*, or marriage canopy. As the couple met in private to consummate the marriage, the friend of the bridegroom stood near their room and was the first to hear the words of the bridegroom as he bragged on his lovely bride.

In John 3:29, John the Baptist claimed he was the friend of the bridegroom. The law and the prophets were until John, but John's ministry introduced the ministry of Christ to the world. John's message was to repent of your sins for the kingdom of heaven is at hand (Matthew 3:2). After John's death, Christ continued proclaiming this theme that the kingdom of heaven was at hand. John actually died under the Mosaic Law; however, Paul spoke of espousing the church to one husband, who is Christ (2 Corinthians 11:2). Both John and Paul are friends of the bridegroom.

THE WEDDING INVITATIONS

Christ gave two important wedding parables, one in Matthew 22:1-14 and the second in Luke 12:35-38. The first parable tells of a king preparing a marriage feast for his son. When the invitation was given, those invited to attend were too busy with earthly cares to come and participate. The king ordered the destruction of these servants, and sent a second invitation into the "highways and hedges" to find a group who desired to attend the wedding.

When reading the parable, we see that the king made one invitation and the servants did not come (Matthew 22:3). After the feast was ready, he sent a second invitation, only to be turned down by his own servants. Luke also bears out this double invitation:

> Then He said to him, "A certain man gave a great supper and invited many, and sent his servant at supper time to say to those who were invited, Come, for all things are now ready'" (Luke 14:16, 17).

The first invitation told of the wedding, and the second invitation confirmed the wedding was ready. The Bible says, "The Spirit and the Bride say come" (Revelation 22:17). The first invitation to the wedding supper is given by the Holy Spirit when we are converted, and the second invitation by the bride. After the invitation, the king saw a man at the wedding without a wedding garment:

> But when the king came in to see the guests, he saw a man there who did not have on a wedding garment. So he said to him, "Friend, how did you come in here without a wedding garment?" And he was speechless. Then the king said to the servants, "Bind him hand and foot, take him away, and cast him into outer darkness; where there will be weeping and gnashing of teeth" (Mathew 22:11-13).

When a king or monarch gave a great supper, it was a custom to enter the large banquet hall and observe each guest that was present. Why was the king so shocked when a person from outside his palace (the "highways and hedges") was seated without a proper garment? If he was a poor person, he could not afford an expensive garment, so what is the meaning of this statement in the parable?

When outsiders came in for a huge supper, it was a custom for the king to have a massive wardrobe from which the visitors could choose a garment to wear. According to the parable, the king had provided the invitation and even the royal garments necessary for the common person to attend the wedding of his son.

God provided for us an invitation to a wedding supper and has clothed us with a heavenly robe of white linen, which we shall wear at the marriage supper of the lamb. Revelation 19:7, 8 says, "Let us be glad and rejoice and give Him glory, for the marriage of the Lamb has come, and His wife has made herself ready. And to her it was granted to be arrayed in fine linen, clean and bright, for the fine linen is the righteous acts of the saints."

The understanding is clear—we are invited, but we must have on the right apparel to attend. The King provides that apparel to us and it is His robe of righteousness. We enter the supper because of His righteousness, not ours!

The Door Was Shut

And while they went to buy, the bridegroom came, and those who were ready went in with him to the wedding; and the door was shut. Afterward the other virgins came also, saying, "Lord, Lord, open to us!" But he answered and said, "Assuredly, I say to you, I do not know you" (Matthew 25:10-12).

Strive to enter in at the straight gate: for many, I say unto you, will seek to enter in, and shall not be able. When once the master of the house has risen up and shut the door, and you begin to stand outside and knock at the door, saying, "Lord, Lord, open for us," and He will answer and say to you, "I do not know you, where you are from" (Luke 13:24, 25).

In the Parable of the Ten Virgins, the bridegroom (the Lord) had delayed His return and the 10 virgins fell asleep. After they awoke, five of them realized they had no additional oil for their oil lamps. The other five had extra oil, but only enough for themselves. As the five foolish virgins ran into the city to buy additional oil, the bridegroom returned and entered the bridal chamber with the bride, shutting the door behind him.

In ancient times, the guests at a large banquet presented their invitations to a servant who was stationed at the door to guard against uninvited persons. In this passage, the door being shut meant the wedding preparations were ready and five were prepared to attend, while five remained outside the door.

In the Book of Revelation, John spoke a prophetic word to the seven churches of Asia, which represent the seven ages of church history. After this, the scene shifts from earth to heaven. John saw a door in heaven and heard a voice saying, "Come up here" (Revelation 4:1, 2). This catching up into heaven is a picture of the coming of the Lord for the church.

When Noah entered the ark and the door was shut, Noah's family was secure from the flood and those on the outside were unable to enter the ark. When the door of heaven opens, the born again believers will be caught up to meet the Lord (1 Thesslonians 4:16, 17). Those who are not ready will remain behind.

NOT IN THE WINTER OR ON THE SABBATH

> But woe to those who are pregnant and to those who are nursing babies in those days! And pray that your flight may not be in winter or on the Sabbath. For then there will be great tribulation, such as has not been since the beginning of the world until this time, no, nor ever shall be (Matthew 24:19-21).

This warning is found in Matthew 24, the discourse listing the many signs of Christ's coming and the end of the age (see vv. 1-3). History now demonstrates that there are certain passages in the text that predict two times of tribulation for Israel. The first is prior to the destruction of Jerusalem and the Temple in A.D. 70, and the latter will occur during the seven-year Tribulation at the end of the age.

Christ instructed those living in Judea to "flee to the mountains" (Matthew 24:16). Christians living in and near Jerusalem before the destruction of the city heeded this warning. When believers saw the Roman legion marching toward Judea, instead of joining the Jewish revolt, they escaped into the mountains and many eventually settled in Pella, where they built a Christian community.

For those who remained, it was a treacherous time. According to Josephus, there was a famine so severe that people were boiling shoe leather in an attempt to eat it, and bandits were invading homes and prying food out of the mouths of anyone fortunate enough to have a few morsels. As always, children were suffering the worst. Christ warned, "Woe to them who are with child and give suck in those days" (Matthew 24:19).

Finally, he told them to pray that the coming invasion would not happen in the winter or on a Sabbath day. Since Judea and Jerusalem are the focal point of the prophecy, Christ knew that winter months could bring huge amounts of snow, because Jerusalem's elevation is 2,500 feet. If the Romans attacked in the winter, the difficulty of escaping would be greater.

Christ told them to pray that it would not be on the Sabbath, for the religious Jews were forbidden by the law to travel long distances on the Sabbath day. According to Acts 1:12, the disciples of Christ traveled a Sabbath day's journey, which was less than a mile. Thus, if the assault began in the winter or on the Sabbath, there was less chance of escaping it.

The same can be said of the future invasion of the Antichrist and his armies. The Antichrist will set up an image of himself which will speak and live through a demonic miracle (Revelation 13:14, 15).

Jews will discern the activity of Satan working through this man, and once again flee to the wilderness for protection (Revelation 12). If their flight is in the winter, they could be caught and slaughtered by the future man of sin, the Antichrist. To this day, religious Jews living in Israel will only travel a Sabbath day's journey on the Sabbath.

The same prophetic warning given to the Jews in the first century is also given to the Jewish remnant during the future seven-year Tribulation. His timeless message is to pray that your escape will not be in the winter or on the Sabbath!

RUNNING TO THE DENS AND CAVES

And the kings of the earth, the great men, the rich men, the commanders, the mighty men, every slave and every free man, hid themselves in the caves and in the rocks of the mountains, and said to the mountains and rocks, "Fall on us and hide us from the face of Him who sits on the throne and from the wrath of the Lamb!" (Revelation 6:15, 16).

As future Tribulation wars and judgments break upon the earth with a vengeance, men will flee from large cities and "head toward the hills." This is the same movement that Lot made moments before Sodom and Gomorrah were erased from the earth. Lot was directed into the mountains to the small city of Zoar (Genesis 19:22-30).

There may be another meaning to the idea of men running to the "rocks of the mountains." In most modern countries, there are underground bunkers built deep within the mountains.

In the mountains of West Virginia, there is an old historic hotel that has a large underground bunker built to use in case of a major nuclear attack on Washington, D.C. This location was a well-preserved secret for many years, but became public after the cold war.

My sources tell me there are also secret bunkers deep within the Smokey Mountains in Tennessee and in areas of Virginia.

When the Tribulation wars begin to impact the nations, men will run to the mountains in an attempt to survive in caves and dens. The Greek word for den is *spelaion*, which means "a cavern, hiding place or resort," which could allude to the many bunkers built by governments in the event of a national calamity.

Except the Days be Shortened

Unless those days were shortened, no flesh would be saved; but for the elect's sake those days will be shortened (Matthew 24:22).

This prophecy about the future Tribulation has puzzled scholars for centuries. We know that the future time of tribulation, called Jacob's trouble (Jeremiah 30:7), Daniel's 70th week (Daniel 9:27), the Tribulation (Matthew 24:29), and the Great Tribulation (Matthew 24:21) is seven years in length.

The Book of Revelation divides this seven years into two halves. The first half is 42 months and the second half, known as the greater Tribulation, is also designated for 42 months (Revelation 11:2 and 13:5). The time frame is so precise that John revealed the exact number of days for each half of this seven year period. The first phase will be 1,260 days and the second phase 1,260 days, totaling a period of seven years (Revelation 11:3 and 12:6).

The perplexing question has been, if the time of Tribulation has already been set and we know the exact number of days, then how could the days be shortened? Some scholars suggest that the actual days will not be shortened, but the persecution itself will be shortened *(Dake's Bible,* New Testament notes, page 27). I want to suggest another possible explanation.

The answer may be found in the type of calendar being used today versus God's prophetic calendar. In ancient times, the calendar was 12 months of 30 days each. The Jews used a lunar calendar based on the cycles of the moon and added an additional month every four years to ensure that the feasts fell in their proper seasons. Later, the entire world accepted a solar calendar consisting of 365.25 days in a solar year. Occasionally a leap year is added to make an entire day out of the .25 part of the day in each year.

An interesting discovery can be made when examining the time of Tribulation using the Biblical numbers in the Book of Revelation. The first half of tribulation is 42 months of 1,260 days on the prophetic calendar. Today, slightly over 1,277 days on the solar calendar make up 42 months. According to calculations in Revelation, the Tribulation is two 42-month periods of 1,260 days each, or a total of 2,520 days in seven years. Today, if I use our solar calendar, there are about 2,556.50 days in a seven-year period.

The solar calendar of today has an additional 36.50 days in seven years than does the prophetic calendar God uses in the Book of Revelation. Thus, the Tribulation still consists of two periods of 42 months, but these are 42 months on God's original prophetic calendar and not time according to our present solar calendar. The Tribulation will be "cut short" about 36 days on our calendar. The reason is because the battle of Armageddon will be so great that if the days were not shortened "no flesh would be saved" (Matthew 24:22).

THE CARCASS AND THE EAGLE

For as the lightning comes out of the east, and shines even to the west; so shall also the coming of the Son of man be. For where ever the carcass is, there will the eagles be gathered together (Matthew 24:27, 28).

When Christ said, "Where ever the carcass is there the eagles would be gathered together," what was He alluding to? The statement prior to this verse speaks of the swiftness of Christ's coming. The passage after this verse says, "Immediately after the tribulation" (Matthew 24:29).

Some individuals who are preterists believe that Matthew 24 was fulfilled prior to and at the time of the destruction of Jerusalem in A.D. 70. Therefore, the "eagles gathered around the carcass" is interpreted to mean that, since the eagle was an emblem of the Roman empire and was placed upon the standards when the Romans went into battle, the eagles allude to the Roman soldiers who gathered around the slain bodies of Jews who did not escape the city.

The main problem with this interpretation is that the previous verse mentions the lighting-fast return of Christ, and two verses later, "Then shall appear the sign of the son of man in heaven" (Matthew 24:30). Using the laws of proper Biblical interpretation, the preterist interpretation does not match the context of the prophecy.

Since Jesus mentioned His coming and the Tribulation, this strange prediction falls in line with an event toward the end of the Tribulation. Revelation 16:16 mentions the Battle of Armageddon. In chapter 19, Jesus returns to earth on a white horse, followed by the "armies in heaven" (v. 14). Christ is returning to earth to do battle against kings, captains and mighty men (v. 18). Prior to the battle at the conclusion of the seven-year Tribulation, an angel of God summons the birds to eat the flesh of the men slain in battle.

> Then I saw an angel standing in the sun; and he cried with a loud voice, saying to all the birds that fly in the midst of heaven, "Come and gather together for the supper of the great God, that you may eat the flesh of kings, the flesh of captains, the

flesh of mighty men, the flesh of horses and of those who sit on them, and the flesh of all people, free and slave, both small and great" (Revelation 19:17, 18).

So many birds of prey attend this supper that their "mouths are filled with the flesh of the armies slain by the brightness of Christ's coming" (Revelation 19:21). There are two Greek words for fowls and both are neutral, meaning the word alludes to any form of a flying bird. When Jesus said "eagles," the Greek word is *aetos*, and is an eagle.

Large ravenous birds are commonly spotted in two locations in Israel. One location is called the abyss, a huge natural ravine carved into the rolling hills of the upper Bashan (Golan Heights). The second location is the area surrounding the mountains near the Valley of Megiddo, the scene of the final global conflict in Revelation 16:16. Several of these large, flesh-eating birds are called eagles. Christ was saying the eagles would gather around the carcasses of men slain in battle at the end of the Tribulation. This is a sign the Son of man will be returning (Matthew 24:30).

THE MARRIAGE SUPPER

Then he said to me, "Write: Blessed are those who are called to the marriage supper of the Lamb!" And he said to me, "These are the true sayings of God" (Revelation 19:9).

In John we read that Jesus and His disciples were invited to a Jewish wedding in Cana of Galilee (John 2:1-10). In Christ's day, the bride was brought to the groom's father's house where a marriage supper continued for seven straight days. Seven days of feasting was a common custom, even in the Old Testament (Judges 14:10-

15). This explains why the host of the marriage supper ran out of wine–the celebration had continued for some time (John 2:3).

The church is identified as a chaste virgin who is espoused (engaged) to Christ (2 Corinthians 11:2). As a virgin, the church will be presented to Christ at His father's house in heaven, where He has prepared a place for us (John 14:1-3). Following our presentation to Christ under the heavenly *chupah*, we will attend the marriage supper of the lamb, which is the consummation of the marriage of God's son to His bride, the church. This wedding supper must take place in heaven, because this is the dwelling place of Christ's father!

If, during the earthly Jewish weddings, the marriage feasts continued for seven days, then we can assume the same pattern fits for the heavenly marriage supper. In fact, the future Tribulation is seven years long and the true church will be in heaven during this entire seven-year period.

Scholars have noted that in Revelation 2 and 3, there are messages to the seven churches; but starting with chapter four, there is no more mention of the church on earth as the wrath of God is being poured out during the seven-year Tribulation.

I believe this is because the church is in heaven receiving rewards (Revelation 11:18), and enjoying the marriage supper of the lamb!

THE KING WITH MANY CROWNS

His eyes were like a flame of fire, and on his head were many crowns; he had a name written that no man knew, except himself (Revelation 19:12).

When Jesus ministered on earth, many people considered Him to be a prophet (Mathew 21:11). After His ascension into heaven, He became the High Priest in the Temple in heaven, ever living to make intercession on our behalf (Hebrews 4:14, 7:25). In the future, Christ will become the King of kings and take possession of the kingdoms of this world (Revelation 19:16).

The first chapter of the Book of Revelation introduces Jesus as the High Priest, wearing a white garment and standing before the seven golden candlesticks (Revelation 1:13). There is no reference to Him wearing a crown, because as long as the High Priest in the Old Testament was operating on the Day of Atonement (*Yom Ha Kippurim*), He was not permitted to wear the gold crown.

In the middle of the Book of Revelation, we see another picture of Christ sitting on a cloud with a golden sickle, and a gold crown on His head (Revelation 14:14). This is a picture of Christ preparing to receive the harvest from the earth. The Feast of Tabernacles is the Jewish feast where seven types of fruit are presented at the Temple. This is called the "ingathering." The High Priest is permitted to wear his gold crown on this day. In Revelation 14, this angel wearing a gold crown represents Jesus, preparing to reap the harvest on earth.

In Revelation 19, toward the end of the Tribulation, Christ has been declared King and has "many crowns" on His head. In the ancient times, when a monarch claimed authority over more than one country, he wore more than one crown. Two historical examples are the kings of Egypt and Ptolemy. Egypt was divided between Upper and Lower Egypt, so the Egyptian kings wore two distinct crowns to signify authority over the two regions of Egypt. When Ptolemy entered Antioch, Greece, he was observed wearing three crowns—two representing his control of Egypt and one for Asia.

The fact that Jesus has no crown in chapter one, but many crowns in chapter 19, reveals that He has successfully conquered the kingdoms of the world through His judgments, and has warred against the armies of the Antichrist and is victorious. He returns as King with the "armies in heaven" to take control of Jerusalem and set up His earthly, visible dominion on earth (Revelation 19:14).

EVERY EYE SHALL SEE HIM

Behold, He is coming with clouds, and every eye will see Him, even they who pierced Him. And all the tribes of the earth will mourn because of Him. Even so, Amen (Revelation 1:7).

Centuries ago, infidels would read this passage and mockingly proclaim the Bible as uninspired Jewish literature. How could every eye see the return of Christ? With millions scattered on seven continents and the earth being 25,000 miles in circumference, it was deemed impossible for this passage to be taken literally.

Modern technology has now made it possible for millions of people to witness the visible return of Christ when He comes to set up His throne in Jerusalem. Through satellite and digital cable technology, news reports can be broadcast around the globe to everyone who has satellite and cable.

As the final battle of Armageddon erupts in the plains of Megiddo, news cameras will carry live images of the violent event. Suddenly, flashes of white light will brighten the heavens near the clouds. As cameramen are instructed to zoom in on the strange unidentified objects hovering in the heavens, the central focus will be Jesus Christ coming on a white horse followed by the armies of heaven (Revelation 19:11-16).

Millions of Americans were glued to their television sets during the war in Iraq as imbedded reporters filmed live, on-location footage. Through these new advanced technologies, people from every nation will be able to receive a live feed of Christ's coming.

They that "pierced Him" alludes to those in Christ's time who were directly involved in His crucifixion. These people will be raised from the dead during a future great white throne judgment, and see firsthand that Christ was raised from the dead and rules as the King of kings and Lord of lords (20:5, 11-14).

GOODBYE TO THE GOATS

And He will set the sheep on His right hand, but the goats on the left (Matthew 25:33).

The Bible uses animals to represent the personality traits or character of people. In the Scriptures, Jesus is pictured as the Great Shepherd who is concerned about His sheep (John 10:11-14). The sheep represent believers who follow Christ, and are obedient to the instructions of the Shepherd. Goats are identified as individuals who are stubborn, rebellious and disobedient.

In the Middle East, sheep and goats are allowed to graze together during the day. They often intermingle while grazing through the pasture. As night approaches, the sheep and the goats are separated. In this parable, Christ illustrates the fact that sheep and goats will be in the same pasture until the end of the age when the Lord himself will separate them. The time of this final separation is set for the beginning of the millennial reign of Christ. Matthew details this event in Matthew 25:31-33:

> When the Son of Man comes in His glory, and all the holy angels with Him, then He will sit on the throne of His glory. All the nations will be gathered before Him, and He will separate them one from another, as a shepherd divides his sheep from the goats. And He will set the sheep on His right hand, but the goats on the left.

This passage alludes to Christ sitting on His throne in Jerusalem immediately after the seven-year Tribulation. The prophet Joel mentions this judgment of the nations in Joel 3:2, which says:

> I will also gather all nations, and will bring them down into the valley of Jehoshaphat, and will plead with them there for my people and for my heritage Israel, whom they have scattered among the nations, and parted my land.

The Valley of Jehoshaphat is located in what is known today as the Kidron Valley, the low ravine that lies just below the Eastern Gate in Jerusalem. At this judgment, Christ will separate the wheat from the tares (Matthew 13:24-30). The wheat represents those who survived the Tribulation and have received Christ as their Messiah. The tares would be those who received the Mark of the Beast or worshiped the image of the Beast, and will not be permitted to live on earth or serve in Christ's kingdom. The imagery of sheep and goats being separated alludes to this judgment in Jerusalem.

THE ROD OF IRON

Three times in the Book of Revelation, the reader is told that Christ will return to earth and "rule with a rod of iron" (2:27, 12:5, 19:15). As a child I visualized Christ in royal apparel, a huge gold crown on His head and a massive iron rod in His hand, beating and slapping down anyone who would do or say anything He did not approve. Perhaps this is your mental image when you hear that He will "rule with a rod of iron."

The word used in the New Testament for a rod of iron means "a stick, a cane, or a rod of royalty." The same Greek word *rhabdos* is used in various New Testament passages and is translated as Aaron's rod (Hebrews 9:4), and a staff used on a journey (Matthew 10:10). In Roman times the soldiers, called sergeants or rodbearers, used iron rods to beat and punish certain people. Paul wrote of being beaten three times with rods (2 Corinthians 11:25).

In ancient times, every king or monarch used a royal scepter. The word scepter is used in a prophecy Jacob gave regarding the coming Messiah. Genesis 49:10 states, "The sceptre shall not depart from Judah, neither a lawgiver from between his feet, until Shiloh comes." As ancient shepherds used their rods to count and comfort sheep (Psalms 23:4), the King-Messiah will use His kingly rod to represent His authority as King of kings over all the earth (Revelation 19:16).

One reason the scepter is called a rod of iron is that during the early part of Christ's reign, there will still be nations not in total subjection to Christ's authority. In fact, some nations will refrain from attending the yearly feast of tabernacles, and God will punish them by withholding the rain in the heavens.

> And it shall come to pass that everyone who is left of all the nations which came against Jerusalem shall go up from year to year to worship the King, the Lord of hosts, and to keep the Feast of Tabernacles. And it shall be that whichever of the families of the earth do not come up to Jerusalem to

worship the King, the Lord of hosts, on them there will be no
rain (Zechariah 14:16-17).

Even during the millennial reign, it will be necessary
for Christ to punish those among the human population
who will not be obedient to the commandments and instructions of the king. This is why His scepter is a "rod
of iron." He is the Prince of peace and King of kings, but
also the Lord of lords (Isaiah 9:6; Revelation 19:16). He
is in charge, and everyone on earth will know it!

The Loosing of Satan

And cast him into the bottomless pit, and shut him up, and set a
seal upon him, that he should deceive the nations no more, till
the thousand years should be fulfilled: and after that he must be
loosed a little season (Revelation 20:3, KJV).

Now when the thousand years have expired, Satan will be released from his prison and will go out to deceive the nations
which are in the four corners of the earth, Gog and Magog, to
gather them together to battle, whose number is as the sand of
the sea (Revelation 20:7, 8).

One of the first questions I recall hearing in Sunday
school class as a child was, "Why would God bind Satan
and then release him on earth again at the end of the
1,000-year reign of Christ?" At first glance, this action
seems ludicrous. If Satan is bound in the abyss, why
not keep him confined for eternity? Why is Satan loosed
for a season?

During the 1,000-year reign of Christ, there will be
two main groups of people living at that time. The first
group will be the saints of God who returned to earth
with Christ from heaven. They will consist of the Old
Testament saints, the New Testament saints and those
raptured at the coming of Christ. The second group will

be people who survived the Tribulation and will be re-populating the earth during the 1,000-year reign.

According to Isaiah, a child born at this time will live to be 100 (65:20). Humans living on earth will again replenish the population during the 1,000-year reign. Satan and his evil spirits will be bound, and men will be brought under submission to Christ, who shall "rule with a rod of iron" (Revelation 19:15). Because Satan is bound, the influence of temptation will be restrained. Men will not be under the demonic influence that has gripped the human mind for 6,000 years.

The loosing of Satan will allow the enemy one more opportunity to test and tempt those who have been born during the millennial reign, in the same manner that humans experienced for 6,000 years prior to the imprisonment of Satan.

Notice how Satan is able to deceive nations and bring an army as numerous as the sands of the sea to besiege Jerusalem. Divine intervention from God interrupts the invasion and Satan is immediately cast into the lake of fire, where his doom is sealed for eternity (Revelation 20:10). The loosing of Satan is one more final test for men living on earth.

THE GREAT WHITE THRONE JUDGMENT

At the conclusion of Christ's 2,000-year reign, the Bible speaks of a judgment in heaven, identified by scholars as the "great white throne judgment." What is this judgment, who will be present, and what will be the end result of those who stand before this throne? The writer of Hebrews said, "It is appointed unto man once to die and after this the judgment" (Hebrews 9:27). Hebrews

226 / U<small>NLOCKING</small> S<small>ECRETS</small> <small>IN THE</small> S<small>ECOND</small> C<small>OMING</small> S<small>CROLLS</small>

6:2 speaks of "eternal judgment." These judgments have no connection to the wrath of God poured out during the Tribulation, often called the judgment of God. These judgments occur in the court of heaven, or before God who is the eternal Judge.

The two main judgments are the judgment seat of Christ and the great white throne judgment. The judgment seat of Christ, called the *Bema*, is where all believers who are resurrected from the dead and raptured when Christ returns for the Church (1 Thessalonians 4:16-17, 1 Corinthians 15:52) will stand and give an account of their words, actions and works while they lived on earth.

> But why do you judge your brother? Or why do you show contempt for your brother? For we shall all stand before the judgment seat of Christ (Romans 14:10).

> For we must all appear before the judgment seat of Christ; that every one may receive the things done in his body, according to that he hath done, whether it be good or bad (2 Corinthians 5:10, KJV).

At this judgment seat our works will be tried in fire, and if our motives were pure and our work for God on earth is honored, we will receive a great reward (1 Corinthians 3:14). Others will be saved but lose their reward because they did not obey God in all things while on earth. "Every man will receive his own reward according to his own labor" (1 Corinthians 3:8).

This Bema judgment occurs in heaven in the middle of the seven-year Tribulation.

> The nations were angry, and your wrath has come, and the time of the dead, that they should be judged, and that you should reward your servants the prophets and the saints, and those who fear your name, small and great, and should destroy those who destroy the earth (Revelation 11:18).

The great white throne judgment occurs at the end of the 1,000-year reign of Christ. The following people will be present at this judgment:

- ♦ Those who accepted the mark of the beast during the Tribulation.
- ♦ Those who died during the Tribulation.
- ♦ Those who lived and died during the 1,000-year reign of Christ.
- ♦ Those who were in hell must stand before God.
- ♦ The angels will be judged.
- ♦ All who have lived from Cain to the end of the 1,000 years.

John tells us that those who were martyred for Christ during the Tribulation will be resurrected and reign with Christ for 1,000 years (Revelation 20:4). John said, "The rest of the dead (were not resurrected) until the thousand years were finished" (Revelation 20:5). At the conclusion of the 1,000-year rule of Christ, all who have died from the time of Adam to the present, and were in hell, will stand before God.

John predicted, "And death and hell delivered up the dead that were in them" (Revelation 20:13). This would also include the numerous fallen angels that are presently bound in *tartarus*, a prison in the lower parts of the earth (2 Peter 2:4). These wicked angels are "reserved unto the judgment of the great day" (Jude 6). At this eternal judgment, Paul predicted, "We will judge the angels" (1 Corinthians 6:3).

At this judgment, individuals will be judged from a series of heavenly books that have recorded each person's deeds, words, and actions during their human lives. The "dead were judged out of the things written in the books"

(Revelation 20:12). I once believed that everyone standing at this judgment was doomed for eternity. However, there will be those who died during the 1,000 year reign who had faith in Christ and if we "judge the angels," it may be possible that certain angels will be rewarded for their obedience.

Those who died with faith in Christ have their names inscribed in the lamb's book of life and will be permitted to enter the New Jerusalem. Those whose names do not appear will be cast into the lake of fire to accompany Satan and his fallen angels (Revelation 20:15).

There is one reason God would bring those in hell before His judgment. In this manner, the Lord can open the books and reveal why those individuals will spend eternity separated from Him. No human spirit will ever accuse God of being unjust towards them. Their own words will either justify or condemn them (Matthew 12:37). So it is far better to be a part of the first resurrection and stand before the Bema than to risk the great white throne.

> Blessed and holy is he who has part in the first resurrection. Over such the second death has no power, but they shall be priests of God and of Christ, and shall reign with him a thousand years (Revelation 20:6).

The Mysterious Holy City

The heavenly Jerusalem existed long before the earthly city of Jerusalem. Paul indicated that Abraham "looked for a city which hath foundations whose builder and maker was God." Thousands of years later, Jesus spoke of heaven and said, "In my father's house are many mansions" (John 14:1-3). Just as the tabernacle of Moses was patterned after heavenly things and the Temple of

Solomon was prepared similar to the Temple of God in heaven, the concept of the ancient city of Jerusalem was patterned after the heavenly Jerusalem.

Revelation 20 and 22 give the reader detailed dimensions of the Holy City. Converted to our present calculations, the city's measurements are 1,500 miles square and 1,500 miles high (Revelation 21:16). We have always assumed the city was a 1,500-mile square, similar to a cube.

Others believe, however, that the city is shaped like a pyramid, with the base being 1,500 miles square and the top (the point of the pyramid) being 1,500 miles high from the ground to the top.

The New Jerusalem has 12 foundations, each consisting of 12 different precious stones (Revelation 21:19-20). These 12 stones are:

- Jasper – the first foundation
- Sapphire – the second foundation
- Chalcedony – the third foundation
- Emerald – the fourth foundation
- Sardonyx – the fifth foundation
- Sardius – the sixth foundation
- Chrysolite – the seventh foundation
- Beryl – the eighth foundation
- Topaz – the ninth foundation
- Chrysoprasus – the tenth foundation
- Jacinth – the eleventh foundation
- Amethyst – the twelfth foundation

John indicates the city has 12 main gates and each is a single, solid pearl (Revelation 21:19). There are three gates on the north, south, east and west sides. Angels are stationed at each entrance, and the names of the 12 tribes of Israel are engraved on the gates. The great street of the city is of pure gold, like transparent glass (Revelation 21:21). The city does not need the sun because the glory of God illuminates every portion of the holy complex (Revelation 21:23).

At the conclusion of the 1,000-year reign of Christ, and following the great white throne judgment, the holy city will come from God out of heaven. There are two opinions about where the city will remain. Some teach it will hover above the land mass and others teach it will literally be located on the earth in a 1,500 square mile piece of land.

After God renovates the earth and creates a renewed heaven and earth, the seas will be dried up, and there will be no large bodies of water separating the continents. Therefore, I believe the city will actually sit on the earth, perhaps in the very area where Israel is situated at this present time.

THE MYSTERY OF THE TREE OF LIFE

In the middle of its street, and on either side of the river, was the tree of life, which bore twelve fruits, each tree yielding its fruit every month. The leaves of the tree were for the healing of the nations (Revelation 22:2).

Blessed are those who do his commandments, that they may have the right to the tree of life, and may enter through the gates into the city (Revelation 22:14).

The mysterious tree of life is mentioned in the first chapters of the Bible and in the concluding chapter of the Bible. The Garden of Eden had many trees, but two trees were set apart: the tree of the knowledge of good and evil and the tree of life. When Adam and Eve partook of the forbidden tree of knowledge, their understanding of good and evil was awakened, requiring God to expel Adam and his helpmate, Eve, from the beautiful paradise.

To protect the tree of life, God stationed a cherub with a burning sword to prevent any access to the tree of life. According to Scripture, if the banished couple were to eat of the tree of life in their sinful condition, they could live forever as sinners without possible redemption (Genesis 3:24).

One of the great Biblical mysteries is what happened to the tree of life. There is no historic record of anyone seeing the angel with the sword or the tree. I asked about the tree of life in Israel and heard a tradition that Jerusalem was once the center of the ancient Garden of Eden. After man's fall, the tree of life was removed to an underground, subterranean chamber and is presently under the eye of a guardian angel.

This concept would make an interesting movie, but the likelihood of it being fact, on a scale of 1 to 10, is about minus five!

According to the Book of Revelation, the tree of life is presently in heaven. Was the tree of life in the Genesis account removed from the garden and planted in the city of God? Or does the Revelation account allude to the "original" tree of life and the tree in the Garden was taken from the heavenly paradise and planted in the earthly paradise?

Various traditions exist regarding what the tree of life was and how the fruit affected Adam and Eve. The fruit from this tree had an amazing effect on Adam as he ate from the tree. His physical body remained renewed and apparently free from any form of sickness and disease. According to John, this is one of the benefits of the tree of life.

The heavenly tree produces 12 types of fruit, a new fruit for each month. Imagine one tree capable of producing 12 different types of fruit! This may be why the number 12 becomes so important in Biblical history, as God prepared His plan of redemption to restore eternal life to a fallen human race:

- 12 types of fruit grow on the tree
- 12 sons of Jacob formed the covenant nation of Israel (Genesis 35:22-27).
- 12 apostles of Christ formed the church (Matthew 10:1).

The leaves of the heavenly tree of life, when eaten, will bring physical healing (Revelation 22:2). There is a "river of life" flowing from the throne of God (Revelation 22:1). On both sides of the river is a tree of life (Revelation 22:2).

All trees and plant life need water and light for nourishment and growth. In this city the glory of God is the light and the river of life provides the water (Revelation 22:1-6). This glorious combination causes the fruit and leaves from the tree of life to bring the healing and sustaining life of God to all who partake of its fruit.

We cannot comprehend the things God has prepared for us (1 Corinthians 2:9-10). Paul took a tour of paradise in heaven, returned to earth, and wrote that he saw things it was not lawful to talk about (2 Corinthians 12:4). Many mysteries of the future remain, but knowledge is increasing through in-depth research and inspiration of the Holy Spirit. Such understanding can be revealed when studying the four cups at Passover.

CHAPTER 11

FOUR CUPS AND THE UNFINISHED MEAL

Then He took the cup, and gave thanks, and gave it to them, saying, "Drink from it, all of you. For this is My blood of the new covenant, which is shed for many for the remission of sins. But I say to you, I will not drink of this fruit of the vine from now on until that day when I drink it new with you in My Father's Kingdom" (Matthew 26:27-29).

Every year on the 14th day of the first month of the year, religious Jews observe Passover. Passover is the first of seven appointed Feasts of Israel (Leviticus 23:5). The Passover, known as *pesach*, originated the night before the famous Exodus of the Hebrews out of Egyptian bondage. The Jews sacrificed a spotless lamb, placed the blood of the lamb on the left, right and upper doorposts, and roasted the lamb for the evening meal (Exodus 12:22). The blood on the outside doorpost of each house prevented the death angel from entering the home and taking the life of the firstborn.

Eating the lamb during the Passover meal initiated healing to their physical bodies. This is indicated in Psalms 105:37, which says, "He brought them forth also with silver and gold: and there was not one feeble person among their tribes." Israel was instructed to keep the Passover each year. As generations passed, a beautiful ceremony was instituted, called the *Seder*, which re-lives the Exodus and tells the story of God's ability to bring His people out of bondage. The Passover is a perfect picture of the death of Christ:

The Passover	The Crucifixion
A lamb was offered.	Christ, the Lamb of God, was offered.
There were three marks of blood on the doorposts.	There were three crosses on Calvary.
The blood restrained death.	Christ's blood defeated death.
The firstborn was spared.	Those who believe are spared.

Eating the lamb brought healing.	The Lord's Supper brings healing.
The lamb was slain at Passover.	Christ was crucified on the eve of Passover.

Most Christians are aware of how the ancient Passover was a picture of the death of Christ. There is another amazing picture found in the Passover Seder. The four cups of wine used at the supper table reveal the future redemption of the believer at Christ's return.

THE FOUR CUPS OF WINE

Four cups of wine are used during the Passover, according to Rabbi Eleazar. The wine is mingled with water because of the children who are present. This is also a prophetic image of Christ, the Lamb of God, who died near Passover. From His crucified body came forth blood and water for our redemption (John 19:34). According to Jewish rabbis, the four cups at Passover correspond to the four promises in Exodus 6:6, 7.

- I will *bring you* out.
- I will (rid) *deliver you* from their bondage.
- I will *redeem you* with an outstretched hand.
- I will *take you* to Me for a people.

These four promises of redemption given to Israel in Egypt are the same four promises of spiritual redemption that Christ has provided for every person who accepts His sacrificial death and resurrection. The New Testament teaches that Jesus has promised *to bring us out* of bondage.

Who gave himself for our sins, that he might deliver us from this present evil world, according to the will of God and our Father (Galatians 1:4).

For ye have not received the spirit of bondage again to fear; but ye have received the Spirit of adoption, whereby we cry, "Abba, Father " (Romans 8:15).

Jesus has also given us a promise *to deliver us*:

Who delivered us from so great a death, and doth deliver: in whom we trust that he will yet deliver us (2 Corinthians 1:10).

Through his death, Jesus came *to redeem* mankind back to God:

Who gave Himself for us, that He might redeem us from all iniquity, and purify unto Himself a peculiar people, zealous of good works (Titus 2:14).

Jesus promised to *take us* to Him:

And if I go and prepare a place for you, I will come again and receive you unto Myself; that where I am, there you may be also (John 14:3).

Christ died to bring us out of the bondage of sin, deliver and redeem us, and eventually to take us to His heavenly home! The four Passover cups reveal this truth in a vivid way, but they reveal much more. The names of the four cups continue to paint a picture of God's plan for mankind.

THE NAMES OF THE FOUR CUPS

Each of the four cups of wine has a name. The first cup is called *the cup of sanctification*. Jesus prayed for His disciples:

For their sakes I sanctify Myself, that they also might be sanctified through the truth (John 17:19).

The second cup is called *the cup of affliction*. Jesus referred to this cup when He prophesied of His sufferings which were to follow. They came shortly after the final supper with His disciples.

> Jesus answered and said, "You do not know what you ask. Are you able to drink the cup that I am about to drink, and be baptized with the baptism that I am baptized with?" They said to Him, "We are able" (Matthew 20:22).

Following the last supper and prior to Christ's crucifixion, He spent hours in deep intercession in the Garden of Gethsemane. The agony was so great that His sweat became as great drops of blood (Luke 22:44). During His prayer, He cried out to God saying, "O, my Father, if it be possible, let this cup pass from me" (Matthew 26:39).

During the actual Jewish Passover, when the father, directing the Seder service, comes to this cup of wine, he takes his finger and dips it in the cup and places a small portion of the wine on the table. This is to remember the plagues in Egypt. I believe this action is a representation of the time when Christ's sweat became great drops of blood (Luke 22:44).

The third cup is called *the cup of redemption*. This would have been the cup Christ drank from after the last supper had concluded. Luke 22:20 says:

> Likewise also the cup after supper, saying, "This cup is the new testament in my blood, which is shed for you."

At the Last Supper when Christ announced He was introducing a new covenant through His blood, He held up this cup.

The fourth cup is extremely interesting because it relates to prophecy. This cup is called *the cup of Hallel,* or praise, also known as the cup of consummation. It has also been identified as the cup of Elijah. Prophetically, this cup is the cup of God's wrath that is poured out in Revelation 16:1. This fourth cup is the one Christ alluded to that we will drink together in the future Kingdom of God:

> But I say to you, I will not drink of this fruit of the vine from now on until that day when I drink it new with you in My Father's kingdom (Matthew 26:29).

As believers, we receive the Lord's Supper, called Communion, during our worship services. As we receive the fruit of the vine and the bread, we are told that we are showing forth the Lord's death until He comes (1 Corinthians 11:26).

We anticipate the glorious time when we will sit down with Christ at the marriage supper of the Lamb and partake of *the cup of consummation,* which is represented as the fourth and final cup at the Passover Seder.

Prophetically, the church is between the third and the fourth cups. The third cup, the cup of redemption, speaks of how Christ brought us out of sin and redeemed us.

> You were not redeemed with corruptible things, like silver and gold, from your aimless conduct received by tradition from your fathers, but with the precious blood of Christ, as of a lamb without blemish and without spot (1 Peter 1:18, 19).

We are presently spiritually redeemed, but are anticipating the moment when this physical body will experience a complete and final redemption at Christ's return. Then this mortal, corruptible body will be clothed in immortality and incorruption (1 Corinthians 15:52-54, Ephesians 1:13, 14). As the church moves from the third cup of redemption, the fourth cup of consummation will be drunk at the marriage supper in heaven.

Three meanings of the fourth cup reveal the three applications it represents to the unbelievers, the Jews and the Christians.

First of all, the fourth cup historically represents the climax of the story of Egypt's judgments. Prophetically, it also alludes to the future wrath of God that will be poured out during the great tribulation. The seven trumpet and vial judgments in the Book of Revelation are a portrait of God's wrath being unleashed upon the nations for killing the saints and prophets, and for rejecting the Gospel. Therefore, the fourth cup becomes a cup of wrath to the unbeliever.

Secondly, to the Jews the fourth cup is also called the cup of the anointing of Elijah. Every Jewish family who celebrates Passover understands the importance of this cup. During the Seder, this cup is the only cup that remains upside down on the table. Before drinking from this cup, a child is often sent to the front door to open it and see if the prophet Elijah is in the street to announce the coming of the Messiah. Elijah was translated alive in a chariot of fire and is expected to reappear at the end of days to announce the coming of the Messiah (2 Kings 2:1-12, Malachi 4:5).

In the middle of the future Tribulation, God will send two witnesses to Jerusalem to minister to a large remnant of Jews. These two prophets are referred to in Revelation 11:1-8. Without question, one of these two men will be the prophet Elijah, who is predicted to appear "before the great and terrible day of the Lord" (Malachi 4:5). To the religious Jews who observe the Torah, the fourth cup alludes to the time when Elijah will appear. It also alludes to a time when Elijah will emerge to proclaim the days of the Messiah.

Thirdly, the fourth cup has a different meaning to the Christians. To the unbeliever it will be a cup of wrath. For the Jew it will be the cup introducing Elijah. *To the Christian the fourth cup is the cup of consummation.* The word *consummation* is to refer to the wedding night of a bride and groom. The church represents the bride of Christ, and Christ is the groom. Our consummation is planned for the marriage supper of the Lamb, toward the conclusion of the seven-year Tribulation.

> "Let us be glad and rejoice, and give Him glory, for the marriage of the Lamb has come, and His wife has made herself ready." And to her it was granted to be arrayed in fine linen, clean and bright, for the fine linen is the righteous acts of saints (Revelation 19:7, 8).

Since this is a wedding supper, it is important to examine the details of the ancient Jewish wedding and discover how the customs of the wedding apply to the prophetic future of the church.

ANCIENT JEWISH WEDDING CUSTOMS AND CHRIST'S RETURN

At the ancient Jewish wedding, when a man selected the girl he desired to marry, the young couple would sit together at a table and drink from a single cup of wine to seal the engagement. This was known as the *kiddushin,* or the betrothal stage. This is what occurred when Christ drank from the cup with His disciples at the Last Supper. Together they were entering into a new covenant, or a marriage contract.

During this ritual, the man would present a marriage contract, called the *ketubah,* which listed the responsibilities and the obligations expected from the bride and the groom. The *ketubah* Christ presented to His church was His word! The New Testament explains what Christ expects from us as His faithful bride.

The third important aspect of the engagement is the purchase price, called the *mohar*, which was the price the man was willing to pay for his bride. Just as every Jewish male had to present the *mohar* during the engagement procedure, Christ gave His very life for us to redeem us to God.

After the initial betrothal, the couple was considered legally married. The young man would depart from the table with the promise that he would prepare a place for his bride and return one day to receive her to him. This is the same promise Christ gave His disciples when He said:

> In My Father's house are many mansions; if it were not so, I would have told you. I go to prepare a place for you. And if I go and prepare a place for you, I will come again and receive you to Myself; that where I am, there you may be also (John 14:2, 3).

Then the young man would return to his father's house. The young woman would veil her face, and select up to 10 young female virgins who were thrilled about her engagement. After returning to his father's house, the future groom would begin building a special room for the couple to live in after he received her.

The bride was to be prepared at all times. Her garments were to be clean and free from spot or wrinkle. She never knew the day or the hour that the young man would return. The father of the groom determined when all things were ready for his son to secretly receive his bride and bring her to the room that was built by his son. This same imagery can be seen in the statements Christ made to His disciples concerning His departure and His future return for them:

- Christ was leaving them to prepare a place for them (John 14:1-2).
- Christ did not know the day or the hour He would return (Matthew 24:36).
- Only the Father knew the day and the hour of Christ's return (Matthew 24:36).
- Christ would return in a day and hour they did not expect (Matthew 24:44).
- They were to watch and pray and not be caught sleeping (Luke 21:36).
- They were to keep their garments always white (Revelation 16:15).
- They were to keep their lamps trimmed and burning (Matthew 25:7).

HERE COMES THE BRIDE

When the father finally gave permission for his son to receive his bride, the young man would often send a group of men to the bride's house to announce, "The bride-groom is coming, make yourself ready!" This is what Christ alluded to in the Parable of the Ten Virgins, when the ten virgins heard the call at midnight that the bride-groom was coming (Matthew 25:6).

Upon hearing this announcement, the bride would prepare to meet her husband, whom she had not seen in perhaps many months. These secret receivings of the bride would often occur late at night while other family members were sleeping. This is why Christ told us not to sleep, and to remain awake that we will not be left behind when He returns (Matthew 24:42-43).

The next process of the wedding was called the *nisu'in* and was the consummation stage. This is also known as the "home taking." The word *nisu'in* comes from the verb *nasah,* which means "to lift up, bear, to carry away." This term is taken from the Talmudic stipulation that the marriage is not legal until the bride has entered *chupah.*

The word *chupah* refers to the wedding ceremony and the canopy that covers the bridal couple during the formal ceremony. The *chupah* was originally the wedding chamber prepared by the groom.

This ancient custom of the home taking is what the New Testament reveals will happen to the bride of Christ, the church. Christ will suddenly return and receive us; and we will be carried away, or lifted up, to meet Him in the air and be taken to His father's house (1 Thessalonians 4:16, 17; John 14:1, 2).

As the groom received his bride, the couple then returned to his father's house where they consummated the marriage. Often, a group of close friends would follow the bride with 10 staves of oil lamps. This custom is seen in the Parable of the Ten Virgins, where the five wise had additional oil and followed the bride and groom to his father's house. When the door was shut, the marriage was consummated (Matthew 25:10).

THE SEVEN DAYS OF CONSUMMATION

An interesting part of the ancient wedding custom is that once the couple arrived at the groom's house, they entered the wedding chamber to consummate their marriage and spend seven consecutive days together (Judges 14:10-15). After the seven days, they returned to join the guests, who were called the "children of the bride chamber." As indicated throughout this book, the future Tribulation on earth will be seven years in length.

During this final seven years of Tribulation and human government, the church will be in the presence of our bridegroom in heaven at the marriage supper.

> Let us be glad and rejoice and give Him glory, for the marriage of the Lamb has come, and His wife has made herself ready (Revelation 19:7).

At this time, we will drink from the fourth and final cup of consummation! This is the cup that Christ said he would drink anew with us in the kingdom.

> "But I say to you, I will not drink of this fruit of the vine from now on until that day when I drink it new with you in My Father's kingdom" (Matthew 26:29).

Prophetically, the body of Christ has drunk from three of the four cups represented at the Passover. The fourth cup is awaiting us at the marriage supper of the Lamb in heaven!

In the ancient Jewish wedding, at the time of consummation, witnesses stood outside the bridal chamber for the husband to confirm that his bride was a true virgin. The man would present sheets with spots of blood on them to disclose to the family if the woman had remained a virgin during the time she was waiting on him to return (Deuteronomy 22:15-20).

How does this ancient law fit the imagery of Christ and the church consummating the marriage covenant in heaven? If the church is a faithful virgin, then where is the token of our virginity?

The answer is the fact that the cup we will drink at the marriage supper represents the blood of Christ that was shed to give us access to God and the promise of heaven. His blood made us worthy to enter the kingdom! There is no other way to God.

THE FOUR ALLELUJAHS SHOUTED BY THE ELDERS

Revelation 19 says that as the marriage supper is being prepared, four Alleluias are announced in heaven. This word *Alleluia* is the Greek form of the Hebrew word Hallelujah, which means "praise the Lord." These four "praise the Lord" announcements are spoken by the 24 elders who are sitting on thrones in the throne room of God in heaven. These four Alleluias have a connection to the four cups at Passover.

The first Alleluia is recorded in Revelation 19:1, 2:

> And after these things I heard a loud voice of a great multitude in heaven, saying, "Alleluia! Salvation and glory and honor and power belong to the Lord our God! For true and righteous are His judgments, because He has judged the great harlot who corrupted the earth with her fornication; and He has avenged on her the blood of His servants shed by her."

The second Alleluia is found in verse three:

> Again they said, "Alleluia. Her smoke rises up forever and ever!"

The third Alleluia is found in verses four and five:

> The twenty-four elders and the four living creatures fell down and worshiped God who sat on the throne, saying, "Amen! Alleluia!" Then a voice came from the throne, saying, "Praise our God, all you His servants and you that fear Him, both small and great."

The fourth Alleluia is found in verses six and seven:

> And I heard, as it were, the voice of a great multitude, and as the sound of many waters and as the sound of mighty thunderings, saying, "Alleluia! For the Lord God Omnipotent reigns! Let us be glad and rejoice and give Him glory, for the marriage of the Lamb has come, and His wife has made herself ready."

THE FOUR CUPS AND THE FOUR ALLELUIAS

The four cups of wine used at the Passover Seder reveal the entire plan of redemption from the Cross to the consummation at the marriage supper. The four alleluias fall in line with the same order of the four Passover cups!

The first cup of wine is the cup of sanctification. The common word *sanctify* means "to set apart for a holy purpose." The New Testament word means to purify and is often translated in the English Bible as holiness. Just as God separated the false gods of Egypt from the true God of the Hebrews, we see the Lord in Revelation 19:1 with this Alleluia. This first "praise the Lord" worships God for separating the false Babylonian religion from the true religion found only in Jesus Christ!

The second cup is the cup of affliction. At the second alleluia, the smoke of Mystery Babylon is reaching into heaven. Just as God afflicted the Egyptians with ten plagues for resisting His plan of deliverance for the Jews, Mystery Babylon will receive plagues and judgments in one hour as a result of its treatment of the saints and prophets (Revelation 18:4-8).

Just as the Egyptians attempted to slay the male infants among the Hebrews, Mystery Babylon, the final false religious system on earth, slew the righteous (Exodus 1:16; Revelation 17:6).

The third cup is the cup of redemption. The third alleluia is linked to the church's freedom from the world's false religion. Just as the Hebrews came out of Egypt rejoicing in their redemption, the saints and prophets in heaven are told to rejoice over the destruction of the great religious harlot. God will bring His vengeance upon this religious prostitute.

Finally, the fourth cup is the cup of consummation. This fourth alleluia is linked to the fourth cup of Passover. The fourth cup of consummation will be drunk anew in the kingdom and, along with the fourth alleluia and the 24 elders, will announce the marriage supper of the Lamb in heaven!

By examining Biblical symbolism, patterns, types and shadows, it is clear that God has imprinted future prophetic events within the Scriptures. Such is the case with the four cups of wine used during the Passover Seder. Another marvelous pattern emerges when we study how future prophetic events are hidden in Old Testament stories. The next chapter will reveal how the future was actually encoded in the past.

CHAPTER 12

THE BEGINNING REVEALS THE ENDING

That which is has already been, and what is to be has already been; and God requires an account of what is past (Ecclesiastes 3:15).

Remember the former things of old, for I am God, and there is no other; I am God, and there is none like Me. Declaring the end from the beginning, and from ancient times things that are not yet done, saying, "My counsel shall stand, and I will do all my pleasure" (Isaiah 46:9, 10).

Some inhabitants of the ancient world believed time moved in cycles, and that there were periods of history where events repeated themselves. Perhaps you have heard the cliché that things always come full circle. This is what the writer of Ecclesiastes meant when he wrote:

> That which has been is what will be, that which is done is what will be done, and there is nothing new under the sun (Ecclesiastes 1:9).

As I have demonstrated in this book, past events can be a pattern for the future. Even secular history has examples of how past events are a picture of future events. In America's history, there is no greater example of how history repeats itself than in the presidencies of Abraham Lincoln and John Kennedy. I documented this somewhat bizarre piece of history in my book *Plucking the Eagle's Wings*.

- Lincoln and Kennedy were elected 100 years apart.
- Lincoln was elected in 1860, Kennedy in 1960.
- Both of their Vice Presidents were named Johnson: Andrew and Lyndon Johnson.
- Both Vice Presidents were born 100 years apart: Andrew Johnson in 1808 and Lyndon Johnson in 1908.
- Both assassins were born 100 years apart: John Wilkes Booth in 1839 and Lee Harvey Oswald in 1939.
- The names Lincoln and Kennedy each contain seven letters.
- The names John Wilkes Booth and Lee Harvey Oswald each contain 15 letters.

- The names Andrew Johnson and Lyndon Johnson both contain 13 letters.
- Both Vice Presidents were southern Democratic senators before becoming President.
- Both presidents had their election contested.
- Both were involved with Civil Rights.
- Both presidents were U.S. Senators before becoming presidents.
- Both were shot on a Friday.
- Both were fatally shot from behind in the back of the head.
- Both were shot in the presence of their wives.
- Both had a child to die while they were in the White House.
- Lincoln had a secretary named Kennedy; Kennedy had a secretary named Lincoln.
- Both secretaries warned the presidents not to go to the theater or to Dallas.
- Southern radicals shot both presidents.
- Lincoln was shot from a theater and the assassin hid in a warehouse. Kennedy was shot from a warehouse and the assassin hid in a theater.
- Both assassins were killed before they stood trial.
- Both Vice Presidents were from the south.

This terrible, tragic repeat of history takes an even stranger and more ominous twist when you consider that Lincoln was shot in the Ford Theater and Kennedy was shot in a Ford/Lincoln limousine! The ironies of history cannot be explained except by God.

In the Scriptures

The Bible contains countless examples of how prophetic events that are predicted to occur in the future are hidden in symbols, words, phrases or actual stories in the Old Testament. The Old Testament is the New Testament concealed, and the New Testament is the Old Testament revealed!

Jesus declared He was the Alpha and Omega, the Beginning and the End (Revelation 1:8). Alpha is the first letter of the Greek alphabet and omega is the last letter of the Greek alphabet. Jesus is the beginning and the end of all things. In reality, the beginning and the end are the same.

The Lord instructed the prophet Isaiah to remember the former things. The Lord told him, "I am God . . . declaring the end from the beginning" (Isaiah 46:9, 10). Those things that God would have us to know about the time of the end were revealed to us in the beginning—not just in prophecy, but also in patterns. These truths are often hidden in the stories of the Torah.

In fact, many of the future prophetic events predicted in the New Testament are actually concealed in the Book of Genesis, the first book of the Bible. The name "Genesis" in Hebrew is *Bereshith*, meaning "first in order or beginning." An example of how Biblical history repeats itself is found when solving this seven-part riddle:

1. Without a miracle in his mother's womb, his birth would have been impossible.
2. As an infant, he was called the Son of God.
3. He was carried to Egypt where he was saved from death.

4. He returned from Egypt with signs and wonders.

5. He experienced much sorrow and grief.

6. He was slain by his enemies.

7. He was brought back from death and is alive today.

Perhaps you think this riddle refers to Jesus. I am actually speaking of the birth of Isaac, and the nation of Israel! Without a miracle, his barren mother, Sarah, could not have conceived (Genesis 18:10-14). As an infant nation, Israel was taken to Egypt and spared from famine (Genesis 50:20).

Israel returned from Egypt with signs and wonders and retook the land in the Book of Joshua. Israel experienced much sorrow and grief, was eventually slain by the Roman army in A.D. 70, and ceased to be a Jewish nation. After 1,800 years of being dispersed, Israel was reborn in 1948, and is still alive today!

This riddle alludes to Israel but it also applies to Jesus Christ.

- Without a miracle in the Virgin Mary's womb, Christ could never have been born.
- Even as an infant, He was called the Son of God (Luke 1:35).
- He fled to Egypt where His life was spared from King Herod's death squads (Mathew 2:13-15).
- He returned from Egypt and settled in Israel and preached with signs, wonders and miracles (Acts 10:38).
- The Roman soldiers executed Him, but on the third day, He arose from the dead and is alive today!

This amazing parallel linking ancient Israel and Jesus Christ continues when analyzing the patterns of Israel's early history and the earthly ministry of Jesus Christ.

The Nation of Israel	Jesus
Born in the Promised Land	Born in the Promised Land
Taken suddenly to Egypt	Taken suddenly to Egypt
Baptized in the Red Sea	Baptized in the Jordan
In the wilderness 40 years	In the wilderness 40 days
Returned in the power of God	Returned in the power of the Spirit
12 tribes were birthed	12 disciples were chosen
A new nation was born	A new nation (the church) was born
The Law came at Pentecost	The church was born at Pentecost
3,000 died worshiping the cow	3,000 were saved at Pentecost

The concept that the end will be as the beginning is also evident when studying the beginning and conclusion of Christ's ministry. In the beginning of Jesus' ministry, there was a man named Simon (Matthew 4:18), his mother's name was Mary (1:18), and Mary's husband was named Joseph (v. 16).

A king named Herod was ruling at that time (2:1-22). Forty-two months later, at the conclusion of Christ's ministry, a man named Simon carried the cross (27:32).

There was another Mary called Magdalene (v. 61), a rich man named Joseph of Arimathaea (v. 57), and another king who was also named Herod (Luke 23:7).

The parallel between the beginning and the end is also evident at the beginning of Christ's ministry and His death. At the start of Christ's ministry, Satan challenged Jesus to prove He was the Son of God. In Matthew 4:3, Satan said, "If You are the Son of God, command that these stones become bread," and in verse 6 he took him to the top of the Temple and said, "If You are the Son of God, throw Yourself down."

At the conclusion of Christ's ministry, unbelievers standing at the foot of the cross also repeated this challenge. His enemies began to challenge Him to demonstrate that He was the Son of God: "If You are the Son of God, come down from the cross. Let [God] deliver Him now if He will have Him; for He said, "I am the Son of God" (Matthew 27:40, 43).

The challenge at the beginning and the end of Christ's public ministry was the same—to prove He was the Son of God! The assaults at the beginning and end of Christ's ministry were identical. Many other parallels are evident in Christ's ministry.

At the initiation of His ministry, Christ was identified as the "Lamb of God" (John 1:29). At the conclusion of His ministry, He died as the Lamb of God near the time of Passover, when countless little lambs were being slain at the Temple (John 18:39).

The death of Jesus occurred in Jerusalem at the end of His earthly ministry. His resurrection introduced His new High Priestly ministry in Jerusalem (John 19:41, 20:17). At Christ's death there was an earthquake. When He arose there was an earthquake. His return will initiate an earthquake on the Mount of Olives (Matthew 27:51, 28:2; Zechariah 14:4).

Christ began His ministry with a 40-day fast, and concluded His earthly walk by showing Himself alive for 40 days (Mark 1:13, Acts 1:3). Christ concluded His earthly ministry by ascending to heaven from the Mount of Olives in Jerusalem. He will begin His 1,000-year reign in Jerusalem when He returns to the Mount of Olives (Acts 1:12, Zechariah 14:4).

Christ's ministry is just one example of the Biblical concept of what has been is what will be and how past events contain patterns for the future.

THE TORAH CONTAINS THE FUTURE

In the late 1980's, I hosted a tour group to Israel. Late one evening we were escorted into a secret excavation that was parallel to the Western Wall. The rabbi, a young Jew originally from Canada, told our group that Israeli researchers had discovered coded messages in the Book of Genesis. (Ten years later, this information would be released and published as the Bible Codes). He declared that Almighty God had encoded the entire history of the world within the Torah—the first five books of the Bible.

The rabbi proceeded to reveal a particular day in the month of December in which the leader of communist Romania, Nicolae Ceausescu, would be killed. He said this date was hidden in the codes. He also explained that, according to the codes, communism would fall and the Jews from Russia would return to Israel.

I never followed up on how he received this information, but in 1989, on that very day in December the Romanian leader was killed—soon after that, Russian Jews began returning to Israel. The Rabbi's statement, "The future can be found in the Torah," remained in my mind.

Months later, I was in Bulgaria ministering and researching prophetic scriptures when I noted an ancient Babylon in the Old Testament (Genesis 11), and a future Mystery Babylon in the last days (Revelation 17). The kingdom of Babel is first mentioned in Genesis 10:10, when Nimrod planned the kingdom of Babel.

I began to explore the Book of Genesis to see if the stories of the past could reveal the prophecies of the future. I was amazed to discover that if you begin in Genesis 11 and travel back to Genesis 1, the order of future prophetic events revealed in the New Testament is hidden in the words, phrases and stories in each chapter! I call this concept "Hidden Prophecies in Genesis." One example is in the genealogies.

HIDDEN PROPHECIES IN GENESIS

If we begin with Adam and continue to Abraham, we can use the number of years in the genealogies which gives the age of the man when his first son was born. You can see an amazing pattern.

Reference	Father/Son	When Born
Genesis 5:3	Adam/Seth	130 years
v. 6	Seth/Enos	105 years
v. 9	Enos/Kenan	90 years
v. 12	Kenan/Mahalaleel	70 years
v. 15	Mahalaleel/Jared	65 years
v. 18	Jared/Enoch	162 years
v. 21	Enoch/Methuselah	65 years
v. 25	Methuselah/Lamech	187 years
v. 28	Lamech/Noah	182 years

v. 32	Noah/Shem	500 years
Genesis 11:10	Shem/Arphaxad	100 years
v. 10	2 years after the flood*	2 years
v. 12	Arphaxad/Salah	35 years
v. 14	Salah/Eber	30 years
v. 16	Eber/Peleg	34 years
v. 18	Peleg/Reu	30 years
v. 20	Reu/Serug	32 years
v. 22	Serug/Nahor	30 years
v. 24	Nahor/Terah	29 years
v. 26	Terah/Abraham	70 years

* Note: You must also add the two years after the Flood (Genesis 11:10).

Notice the number of years listed in these genealogies. If we add all the numbers from Adam to Abraham, they total 1,948 years. The unique parallel is that from the time of the second Adam, Jesus Christ (1 Corinthians 15:45) to the rebirth of the modern nation of Israel, the total is 1,948 years. Israel was reborn on May 14, 1948. This clearly reveals a divine pattern and reinforces the concept of the past being repeated in the future.

Genesis 10 lists events and formation of nations after the flood of Noah. When we reverse the order of the information, begin with verse 32 and go back to verse 2, we find an amazing pattern of Israel's history hidden in the Genesis record:

HOW GENESIS 10 REVEALS THE FUTURE OF ISRAEL

Genesis 10, Backward

Genesis 1, Forward

v. 32: Earth after the flood   –   Covered with water

v. 31: Shem genealogy   –   Seth genealogy

v. 30: Land of the east	–	Land near Eden
vv. 26-29: Genealogy	–	14 generations (Adam to Eber)
v. 21: Beginning of Shem's family	–	Beginning of Israel as a nation
v. 20: Land of Ham (Egypt)	–	Israel leaves Egypt
v. 19: Canaan Land	–	Israel in Canaan
vv. 15-18 The Canaanite	–	Israel battled the Canaanites
v. 13, 14 The Philistines	–	Israel battled the Philistines
v. 11, 12 Assyria	–	Captured by Assyria
v. 10 Babylon	–	Taken into Babylon
vv. 7-9 Nimrod, King of Babylon	–	Nebuchadnezzar, King of Babylon
v. 6 Four sons of Ham	–	Four kingdoms of bondage
v. 5 Isles of the Gentiles	–	Scattered among the Gentiles
vv. 2,3 Gomer, Gog and Magog	–	War of Gog and Magog

I believe that the way to discover the patterns of the future is to reverse the order. While this concept of examining the verses and chapters in reverse is not systematic theology or taught in schools of theology, I believe it is God's way of encoding the future in the past.

HIDDEN PROPHECIES IN GENESIS

If we use this technique in the Book of Genesis, we begin to see how certain stories, verses or phrases in the first 11 chapters of Genesis reveal the final chapters of mankind's future history. Genesis 1 is the Creation story and Genesis chapter 11 is the beginning of the first global empire. Prophetically, we are seeing the influence of a global world order through the United Nations and the European Union on earth.

If we begin in Genesis 11 and go back to the Creation story, we discover the main events of end-time prophecy parallel those prophecies and predictions in the New Testament!

THE TOWER AND THE GLOBAL GOVERNMENT

Genesis 11 reveals how a Gentile leader named Nimrod united a large group of people to build a large tower that would reach up to heaven. This tower was the beginning of the kingdom of Babel and is a picture of the future global one-world government that men are trying to build.

> Now the whole earth had one language and one speech. And it came to pass, as they journeyed from the east, that they found a plain in the land of Shinar, and they dwelt there. Then they said to one another, "Come, let us make bricks and bake them thoroughly." They had brick for stone, and they had asphalt for mortar.
>
> And they said, "Come, let us build ourselves a city, and a tower whose top is in the heavens; let us make a name for ourselves, lest we be scattered abroad over the face of the whole earth" (Genesis 11:1-4).

During the time period when the tower was built, there was one universal language. The Gentile nations had come together to build a major structure that would reach into the heavens. These globalists were attempting to make a name for themselves with this primitive skyscraper.

It is a perfect picture of the present emphasis being placed on a new world order and the formation of a global government. There is currently an emphasis that mankind must become one in unity through a united governmental, economic and social order. When the European Union (EU) began to form a new united Europe, an artist drew a large picture of the tower of Babel with the stars representing the EU encircling it.

The tower of Babel was a united effort by all men to build together. Genesis 11 is a picture of the coming global government and one world order.

The Dividing of Nations and Earthquakes

To Eber were born two sons: the name of one was Peleg, for in his days the earth was divided; and his brother's name was Joktan (Genesis 10:25).

Genesis 10 contains a clue about what will happen in the future, and it is found in the meaning of the name Peleg. The Hebrew word for *Peleg* means to "split or divide." *Strong's Concordance* says it means "earthquake." Jesus warned that, in the last days, there would be "earthquakes in various places" (Mathew 24:7).

In Peleg's day, the earth was divided. The pre-planned global government pictured in Genesis 11 will emerge for a brief season. In the future, there will be a major division among the Gentile nations. This is clear from the signs in Matthew 24. Christ said, "Nation will rise against nation, and kingdom against kingdom" (v. 7).

Genesis 10 also lists the names of Japeth's sons: Gomer, Magog, Mahdi, Javan, Tubal, Mechech and Tiras. Several of these names are important in prophecy. There will be a future war in Israel, called the war of Gog and Magog (Ezekiel 38, 39), prior to the Tribulation. Many believe this war will be unleashed before the Rapture of the church.

Drunkenness and Immorality

From Genesis 10, we move to Genesis 9, to see if this chapter contains clues that point to future prophetic events. Genesis 9 deals with events following Noah's flood. There are several possible clues that reveal signs prior to the future return of Christ:

> And Noah began to be a farmer, and he planted a vineyard. Then he drank of the wine and was drunk, and became uncovered in his tent. And Ham, the father of Canaan, saw the nakedness of his father, and told his two brothers outside (Genesis 9:20-22).

After years of hard labor preparing the ark and surviving the flood, Noah apparently felt like it was time to "chill out." He planted a vineyard, made wine and became drunk. This reference from the past reminds me of a warning from the future. Prior to Christ's return, men will become spiritually lazy and began to believe the Lord is delaying His coming.

> But take heed to yourselves, lest your hearts be weighed down with carousing, drunkenness, and cares of this life, and that Day come on you unexpectedly (Luke 21:34).

The New Testament warns about becoming careless to the point of drunkenness prior to Christ's return. As it was in the past, so will it be in the future. Today, even some believers are carelessly compromising their convictions by partaking in social drinking.

The second point is where Noah's son, Ham, saw his father's nakedness. Some scholars point out that the word *saw* in this passage does not necessarily mean to see with the eye, but to have a physical desire for. It may be alluding to the thought that when Ham saw Noah drunk, he had a desire to have some form of perverted relationship with his father.

Because of this sin, Noah cursed Canaan, a son of Ham (Genesis 9:25). Canaan was the father of a tribe called the Canaanites who, centuries later, would dwell in the Promised Land. The phrase "Canaan Land" came from the word *Canaanite*. Some of their descendants were inhabitants of the cities of Sodom and Gomorrah!

Homosexuality and drunkenness are two of the strongest sins America and much of Europe are dealing with. Many gay and lesbian couples often meet in gay bars throughout North America and Europe. Genesis 9 contains an allusion to these two bondages that permeate society in these last days.

THE DOVE AND THE OLIVE BRANCH

Moving from Genesis 9, we turn to Genesis 8. The main theme here is the receding waters of the great flood. In this chapter Noah built an altar and worshiped God. Several important parallels are found:

+ Noah and his family are protected in the ark (Genesis 8:1).

+ The ark has a window, and a dove has access in the ark (Genesis 8:6).

+ The dove carried an olive branch, revealing the storm had ended (Genesis 8:11).

In this chapter, the flood has concluded and Noah is seeking evidence that the waters are receding. Noah sent a dove out of the ark's window (Genesis 6:16). In

Hebrew, the word window is *zohar*, and means "light or illumination." In the last days, God is sending light and illumination regarding the prophetic Scriptures. We are told that knowledge would be increased at the time of the end (Daniel 12:4). This spiritual illumination comes from the Holy Spirit (Hebrew 10:32).

The dove eventually took an olive branch into the ark. An olive branch is the universal symbol of peace. Amid the receding, muddy flood waters, the dove found an olive branch. The Bible indicated that the "end shall be with a flood" (Daniel 9:26).

In the midst of the last day trials and storms, we are promised that God will "pour out of My Spirit on all flesh" (Acts 2:17). One of the nine fruits of the Holy Spirit is peace (Galatians 6:16). As we encounter the time of the end, the dove of the Holy Sprit will move across the waters of spiritual turmoil and bring the olive branch of God's peace into our situation.

As this pattern begins to develop, we can see the global government forming (Genesis 11) and the nations being divided as the final shaking begins (Genesis 10). Men will become sexually impure and spend time being idle and becoming drunk (Genesis 9).

Yet, in the midst of the storms and spiritual flood of iniquity, the Lord will be at work pouring out His Spirit (the dove) upon our sons and daughters, who are seeking refuge in the ark, the church (Genesis 8).

EXTENDED GRACE TO PREPARE

From chapter 8, which discloses the activity of the dove, we come to the main theme of chapter 7. This main flood chapter explains the great destruction that has come to earth. God made a strange statement to Noah in this chapter when He said, "After seven days I will cause it to rain upon the earth" (v. 4). The ark was prepared and Noah's family was waiting for the deluge to begin. However, God gave a seven-day grace period before He sent the final destruction.

As previously noted, the seven days gave Noah time to bury his great-grandfather, Methuselah, and experience the normal seven days assigned to grieve for the dead. What is the hidden message for the future in this chapter? This was the chapter where Noah prepared his family and the animals for the ark. This chapter speaks of the final preparation, and how God will still extend His mercy to the world right up to the very moment of Christ's return for the church.

The Bible teaches it is not God's will that any person perish, but that all come to God through repentance (2 Peter 3:9). Peter wrote about Noah building the ark and said that God was longsuffering when the ark was being prepared. God restrained judgment upon mankind during the entire 100 years of the ark's preparation because He desired to see signs of repentance.

Noah was given seven days of grace before the flood, and we will soon enter a small window of grace prior to Christ's return. This grace period is identified in Revelation 2:21 as a "space to repent."

THE SIGNS OF NOAH'S DAY

We move to chapter 6. This chapter reveals many signs in Noah's day prior to the flood. God warned humanity that His "spirit would not always strive with man" (Genesis 6:3). There was also a race of giant men on the earth in that day, and the imagination of man's heart was continually wicked (Genesis 6:4-6). Violence was sweeping the planet and God chose to destroy the earth because of man's wickedness (Genesis 6:6-11).

When comparing a list of the signs from Noah's day, we can see a repeat of history in the days preceding the Lord's coming:

Noah's Day	Before Christ's Return
Wicked imaginations (*Genesis 6:5*)	Seducing spirits (*1 Timothy 4:1*)
Violence on the earth (*Genesis 6:11*)	Wars and fighting (*Matthew 24:6*)
Excessive eating (*Matthew 24:38*	Excessive eating (*Matthew 24:38*)
Drinking (*Matthew 24:38*)	Drinking (*Matthew 24:38*)
Marrying (*Matthew 24:38*)	Marrying (*Matthew 24:38*)

We are certainly seeing the same pre-flood signs from Noah's day being repeated in our day. These signs indicated a flood was coming and the repeat of these signs reveals that the final Tribulation is coming.

THE CATCHING UP IN CHAPTER 5

In the New Testament, the signs of the days of Noah precede the Lord's return (Matthew 24:37). After the signs of the flood in Genesis 6, we explore the main theme of chapter 5—an amazing event. This passage indicates that Enoch, the seventh from Adam, was translated alive into heaven (Genesis 5:24). As previously alluded to, this incident is a picture of the believer being "caught up" at the coming of the Lord for the church (1 Thessalonians 4:16-17).

After thousands of hours of Bible study, I lean toward a pre-Tribulation catching away of the saints. The pattern found in Genesis seems to support this theory. The pre-Tribulation rapture occurs prior to the seven-year Tribulation. Ironically, after Enoch's translation in chapter 5, we see the seven-year Tribulation and the Mark of the Beast pictured in Genesis 4!

THE TRIBULATION THEME

Following the catching away, we see another pattern emerge in chapter 4. First, Cain murders his brother, Abel (Genesis 4:8). After Abel's death, God spoke to Cain and placed a mark on Cain's forehead so anyone finding him would not kill him (Genesis 4:15). Cain was expelled from the garden and traveled "east of Eden" (Genesis 4:16). Later, it is stated than Cain's punishment was sevenfold (Genesis 4:24).

This early incident gives us a preview of the future Tribulation. Just as Cain killed Abel, during the Tribulation some individuals who receive Christ will be martyred for their faith (Revelation 6:9). Just as Cain received a mark on his forehead, during the middle of the Tribulation men will receive a mark in their right hands or foreheads, giving them permission to buy and sell (Revelation 13:16).

Cain was banished from God's presence and moved east of Eden. Toward the conclusion of the Tribulation, the kings of the east will arise and become a strong force to be reckoned with (Revelation 16:12). Cain's punishment was sevenfold and the world's period of punishment will be seven years. The ancient history of Cain and his descendants gives an early preview of the final seven-year Tribulation. As an additional note, one of Cain's descendants was Lamech. Lamech was the first polygamist in the Bible, and was guilty of murdering a man.

Lamech said, "If Cain's punishment is sevenfold, then my punishment will be seventy and sevenfold" (Genesis 4:24). Seventy multiplied by seven times totals 490. This small passage is unique because Daniel chapter nine has the prophecy of Daniel's 70 weeks:

> Seventy weeks are determined upon thy people and upon thy holy city, to finish the transgression, and to make an end of sins, and to make reconciliation for iniquity, and to bring in everlasting righteousness, and to seal up the vision and prophecy, and to anoint the most Holy (Daniel 9:24).

These 70 weeks are not weeks of days, but weeks of years. Scholars note that the 70 weeks are a prophecy involving 490 years. Genesis 4:24 speaks of 70 times seven, and the prophetic time for Israel was 70 times seven! Without a doubt, chapter 4 gives us clues concerning the time of the end that would be revealed hundreds and, in some cases, thousands of years after the story of Cain and Abel.

Since that which has been is that which shall be, the order of events is reversed as I have been demonstrating. This would place the rapture of the saints just before the seven-year Tribulation. Here is a summary of chapters four and five compared to the order of events found in the New Testament.

Genesis Account	New Testament Prediction
Enoch is translated.	The church is translated.
The Tribulation begins.	The Tribulation begins.
Cain punished 7-fold.	The Tribulation is 7 years.
Cain receives a mark on his head.	Men receive a mark on their heads or hands.

Cain slays a righteous man.	Men who receive Christ are beheaded.
Lamech's punishment was 70 times.	Daniel's 70th week is fulfilled.

THE DEFEAT OF THE SERPENT

In Genesis 3, Satan came into the Garden using a serpent (Genesis 3:1-4). In Revelation 12, Satan is called "that old serpent" (Revelation 20:2). The principle of "what was is what will be" is visible again. In the beginning he came as a serpent and at the end he appears as a serpent. The defeat of Satan is demonstrated in Revelation 20, when an angel binds him in chains and casts him into the abyss (Revelation 20:2, 3). The prediction of Satan's demise is recorded in Genesis 3:15, shortly after Adam and Eve's sin:

> And I will put enmity between you and the woman, and between your seed and her Seed; he shall bruise your head, and you shall bruise his heel.

Following the seven-year Tribulation, the seed of the woman, the Messiah, Jesus Christ, will return to earth to set up His kingdom in Jerusalem. At this time, the serpent (Satan) will be crushed and defeated.

THE 1,000-YEAR REIGN

As we continue to follow the patterns of prophecy, the next main event after Satan is bound will be the 1,000 year reign of Christ on earth as the King of kings and Lord of lords (Revelation 20:4). This 1,000-year time frame may be alluded to in Genesis 2. This chapter gives us a picture of the perfect creation prior to the fall of Adam and Eve. The entire earth was in unity and at peace. Everything was good.

> And on the seventh day God ended His work which He had done, and He rested on the seventh day from all His work which He had done (Genesis 2:2).

Prophetically, the seventh day speaks of the seventh millennium when Christ will set up His kingdom for 1,000 years. The perfection of Genesis 2 is a picture of the perfection of the future Kingdom of the Messiah. The wolf will lie down with the lamb, and men shall beat their swords into plowshares (Isaiah 11:6, 2:4). The serpent and his deception were not present in Genesis 2, and neither will Satan's influence be present during the millennial reign!

ETERNAL PERFECTION

After Satan is bound (Revelation 20:1, 2), and following the millennial reign, there will be a renewed heaven and a renewed earth (Revelation 21:1). John described the holy city, New Jerusalem, coming down from God out of heaven (Revelation 21:2). The time following the 1,000-year reign of Christ is eternity.

In Genesis 1, everything was perfect. Seven times God said it was good (vv. 4, 10, 12, 18, 21, 25, 31). The last two chapters of the Book of Revelation portray eternal perfection. The first two chapters in Genesis are a blueprint of perfection. The first is the same as the last, and the conclusion the same as the beginning.

Genesis 1, 2	*Revelation 21, 22*
There was no sin.	There is no sin.
There was no pain.	There is no pain.
There was no sorrow.	There is no sorrow.

There was no death.	There is no death.
God walked with man.	God walks with man.
Everything was perfect.	Everything is perfect.
Man ate from the tree	We eat from the tree
of life.	of life.

These "hidden prophecies" in Genesis support the theory that things that have been are the things that shall be. To summarize, compare the first 11 chapters in Genesis with events predicted for the future:

In the Beginning	*At the End*
♦ The days of Noah	Signs of the days of Noah
♦ The catching away of Enoch	The catching away of the church
♦ Cain's sevenfold punishment	The seven-year Tribulation
♦ Mark on Cain's head	Mark of the Beast
♦ 70-times-7 judgment	70 weeks of Daniel (70 times 7)
♦ The defeat of the serpent	The binding of the serpent (Satan)
♦ The perfection in the Garden	The perfection of the millennial reign
♦ The perfection of earth	New heaven and new earth

Adam was called the son of God and lived in paradise on earth (Luke 3:38). At the time of the end, the second Adam, Jesus Christ the Son of God (1 Corinthians 15:45), will initiate a new paradise on earth and will restore man to the original perfection of Eden. This is the prophecy of "restitution of all things spoken of by all the holy prophets before the world began" (Acts 3:21).

CONCLUSION

If, after reading this book, people still believe there will not be a return of Christ, then their spiritual ignorance has overcome their common sense. The Scriptures are clear and patterns have been set that reveal Christ will return for the church and return to the earth to set up a visible kingdom for 1,000 years, in Jerusalem.

As the sands in God's hourglass empty toward the end of the age, more visible signs of Christ's return will become evident. Prophetic scholars, teachers, and students will open the Scriptures and study their pages to examine the prophecies in light of present events. Their goal will be to determine if the news before them was revealed through the inspired prophets of the Holy Bible.

Just as the ancient prophets diligently searched the scrolls of prophecy to determine the time of Christ's first appearance, we will continue to search and announce fresh insight and new illumination to help answer the question, "When shall be the signs of His coming?"

Hopefully, what you have read in this book has answered this question in part.

THE MOST IMPORTANT PAGE

The message of the gospel of Jesus Christ can be summed up in three powerful statements:

- Jesus Christ was the Son God and was born of the Virgin Mary.
- Jesus was crucified as the perfect sacrifice to forgive your sins.
- Jesus was raised from the dead and is now in heaven as our High Priest.

When a person believes these three truths, it opens the door for the free gift of salvation. As the Bible says:

> If you confess with your mouth the Lord Jesus and believe in your heart that God has raised Him from the dead, you will be saved. For with the heart one believes unto righteousness, and with the mouth confession is made unto salvation (Romans 10:9, 10).

Salvation is receiving by faith through believing in Christ, asking Him to forgive your sins, and confessing with your mouth that He has saved you from sin. From that moment forward, you must learn more about Jesus through the preaching and teaching of God's word. It is important to find a local church where you can be around other believers and grow in the knowledge of the Lord.

Here is a simple prayer you can pray:

Dear Lord Jesus, I know that I am a sinner. I know you died for me, and because of You my sins are forgiven and I can have a brand new beginning. Today I am asking you to forgive me of my sins and cleanse me through the sacrifice of your death. Today I receive you into my life and from this day forward I will learn your word, trust you, and follow you as you direct my life. I ask this in Jesus name.

If you have prayed this prayer to become a believer, please write us a letter so that we may rejoice with you!

Perry Stone, Jr.
P.O. Box 3595
Cleveland, TN 37320

BIBLIOGRAPHY

Albert Barnes, *Barnes' Notes on the Old and New Testaments*. Grand Rapids, MI: Baker Book House, 1982.

Book of Jasher. Muskogee, OK: Artisan Publishers, 1988.

Bullinger, E.W. *Witness of the Stars*. Grand Rapids, MI: Kregel Publications, 1984.

Dake, Finis. *The Dake Annotated Reference Bible*. Lawrenceville, GA: Dake Publishing.

Encyclopedia Judaica. 16 vols. Jerusalem: Keter Publishing House.

Freeman, James M. *Manners and Customs of the Bible*. New Kensington, PA: Whitaker House, 1996.

Jeffrey, Grant. *Triumphant Return: The Coming Kingdom of God*. Toronto: Frontier Research Publications, 2002.

Lightfoot, John. *A Commentary on the New Testament from the Talmud and Hebraica*. 4 vols. Peabody, MA: Hendrickson Publishers, 1989.

Metzger, Bruce, ed. *The Apocrypha of the Old Testament Revised Standard Version*. New York: Oxford University Press, 1977.

Mordachai, Avi ben. *Signs in the Heavens*. Colorado Springs, CO: Millennium 7,000 Communications, 1997.

Roberts, Alexander, and Donaldson, James, eds. *The Ante-Nicene Fathers*. Grand Rapids, MI: Wm. B. Eerdmans, 1989.

Rodwell, J.M., trans. *The Koran*. New York: Random House, 1993.

Schmaltz, Reuven E. and Raymond R. Fischer. *The Messianic Seal of the Jerusalem Church*. Tiberias, Israel: Olim Publications, 1999.

Soncino Classics Collection. English translation of the Talmud, Midrash Rabbah, and Zohar. London: Soncino Press, 2001. CD-ROM.

Stone, Perry. *Israel Racing Toward the Second Coming*. Voice of Evangelism, 2000, videocassette.

Stone, Perry. *Plucking the Eagle's Wings*. Cleveland, TN: Voice of Evangelism, 2001.

Stone, Perry. *The Rapture Revelation*. Voice of Evangelism, 2002, videocassette album.

Stone, Perry. *Unleashing the Beast*. Cleveland, TN: Voice of Evangelism, 2003.

Unger, Dominic J., trans. *Irenaeus of Lyons: Against the Heresies* (Ancient Christian Writers, No 55). Mahwah, NJ: Paulist Press, 1992.

Vine, W.E. *Vine's Expository Dictionary of New Testament Words*. Peabody, MA: Hendrickson Publishers, 1993.

Whitson, William, trans. *Josephus: The Complete Works*. Grand Rapids, MI: Kregel Publications, 1978.

Wadsworth, Bob. *Biblical Astronomy*. www.atlbible.org/astronomy/astronomy1.htm.

MINISTRY INFORMATION RESOURCE PAGE

We welcome you to contact our ministry for additional information or resource materials, such as books, videos, audio cassettes, CDs, and other informative study tools. You may request a free product catalog by contacting us.

Voice of Evangelism Ministry
P.O. Box 3595
Cleveland, TN 37320

Phone: (423) 478-3456
Fax: (423) 478-1392
Monday to Friday, 9 a.m. to 5 p.m. EST

www.perrystone.org

You can ask about:
♦ Becoming a partner with our ministry through the Partner Strike Force
♦ Joining our 7-a-Month Tape Club
♦ Learn about our yearly conferences and main event camp meetings
♦ Receive information about our annual Holy Land Tour

Our ministry operates on the Philippians 4:19 principle.

ABOUT THE AUTHOR

DR. PERRY STONE, JR., INTERNATIONAL EVANGELIST AND FOUNDER OF THE VOICE OF EVANGELISM OUTREACH MINISTRIES, HAS A RICH MINISTRY HERITAGE AS A FOURTH-GENERATION MINISTER OF THE GOSPEL.

HE BEGAN PREACHING AT THE YOUNG AGE OF 16, CONTINUED HIS EXTERNAL STUDIES THROUGH LEE UNIVERSITY, AND EVENTUALLY EARNED A BACHELOR OF THEOLOGY DEGREE FROM COVENANT LIFE CHRISTIAN COLLEGE. HE HAS ALSO RECEIVED TWO HONORARY DOCTORATES—ONE FROM THE WESLEY SYNOD (TOLEDO, OHIO), AND AN HONORARY DOCTOR OF PHILOSOPHY IN CHRISTIAN SCIENCE FROM SAINT THOMAS-A-BECKETT EPISCOPAL SYNOD OF CANTERBURY, ENGLAND.

THE VOICE OF EVANGELISM HAS MANY BRANCHES OF OUTREACH, INCLUDING A SEVEN POINT OUTREACH FOR GLOBAL EVANGELISM. REVEREND STONE WRITES AND PUBLISHES A BI-MONTHLY MAGAZINE, AND HAS WRITTEN AND PUBLISHED 22 BOOKS, INCLUDING THREE BEST SELLERS.

DR. STONE HAS PRODUCED AN EXTENSIVE LIBRARY OF AUDIO TEACHING ALBUMS AND VIDEOS ON A WIDE VARIETY OF SUBJECTS. HE ALSO HOSTS THE WEEKLY TELEVISION PROGRAM *MANNA-FEST*, WHICH IS AIRED NATIONWIDE ON OVER 500 STATIONS AND SATELLITE TELEVISION. THE MINISTRY IS HEADQUARTERED IN CLEVELAND, TENNESSEE, AND OPERATES OUT OF A 25,000-SQUARE-FOOT MINISTRY CENTER.

PERRY RESIDES IN CLEVELAND WITH HIS WIFE, PAM, AND THEIR TWO CHILDREN.